# MEMORIES
## from the
# MOUNTAINS

*A collection of short stories by a twin girl
comparing life in a small paper town
to country life.*

*1998*

*Josephine Paxton Green*

# Josephine
# Paxton Green

WORLDCOMM
a division of Creativity, Inc.

Publisher: Ralph Roberts
Vice-President: Pat Roberts

Editors: Barbara Blood, Gayle Graham, Susan Parker

Cover Design: Gayle Graham
Interior Design & Electronic Page Assembly: **WorldComm**®

10  9  8  7  6  5  4  3  2  1

Library of Congress Catalog Card Number: 98-61140

ISBN  1-56664-137-3

**WorldComm**®—a division of Creativity, Inc.—is a full–service publisher located at 65 Macedonia Road, Alexander NC 28701. Phone (828) 252–9515, Fax (828) 255–8719.

**WorldComm**® is distributed to the trade by Alexander Books™, 65 Macedonia Road, Alexander NC 28701. Phone (828) 252–9515, Fax (828) 255–8719. For orders only: 1-800-472-0438. Visa and MasterCard accepted.

This book is also available on the internet in the **Publishers CyberMall**™. Set your browser to http://www.abooks.com and enjoy the many fine values available there.

# Contents

## III.

### IV.

**On the cover:**

Upper Left: The house in the center of the picture is where Jo was raised. To the left at the top is the top of the library where Pennsylvania Avenue School used to be. The bottom right is the First Baptist Church of Canton which she attended.

Upper right: Champion Mill

Lower left: The road in the country that ran in front of the house that Jo lived in. (Willis Cove Road.)

Lower right: Park Street in Canton. The Bus stop or "Soda Shop" was in the center of the picture where the ABC Store is today.

# Dedication

I dedicate this book to James Lloyd Wood (Jim), my son who requested me to write these memories and to the family of G.C. Paxton and Annie Jones Paxton and also to the family of Hattie Robinson Wood and Lloyd Wood. If it wasn't for them these memories couldn't happen.

*Which is which?? Standing for company comparison.*

# Preface

Our story unfolds on a cold January night with the birth of twin girls. My sister and I were born during the Depression of 1929, born at home with our hometown doctor in attendance. His son will play a part in my story later on. The doctor lived three houses over from ours in a neat residential area.

Our house was also close to the grammar school. When we were born, the first grade was allowed to come see us as a group. One of the people who was in the group told me they were ushered in, single file, to view us. They came in the front door, saw the babies, and went back to school through the back door. As we grew, when visitors came to our house, we were called out to stand together to be viewed and compared for looks—as to which parent we favored. This I'm sure made us feel a little special which in turn spoiled us. I personally did not like being a twin. It made me feel different from everyone else. I just wanted to be me. Being a twin knocked us out of a lot of things.

We learned to skate at an early age and the streets were worn slick with the neighborhood kids skating on them. My brother, Buzz, bought us our skates by working at the local hardware store. Traffic avoided us when we skated because sometimes we would have eight or nine kids skating. No TV for us—just lots of fresh air and sunshine. We stayed outside all the time, until 10 o'clock at night in the summer time. We also wore out several rope swings. Behind our house was a long stretch of grape vines that my older brother had planted. We played under them and it would be dark

*Right: The Pennsylvania Avenue School. Bottom: The school children were brought from the school through the trees to the left to the house at the right. They were marched single file and back to the school.*

*Pennsylvania Avenue where we skated up and down the street. Grammar school was to the upper right of the picture beyond the pine trees. The trail the kids took to come to see us is by the house near the red truck.*

*Our new white overalls*

under there. We also played house by laying out a house plan from rocks and pieces of coal. We would have a living room, bedrooms and a kitchen. We would play with our dolls in the playhouse for hours on end. As children, we had a pair of white overalls and I have a picture of us with a dog in our arms in the area of our play-house.

Another doctor lived across the street from our house. He was the age of one of my brothers. He had a son a few years younger than us. We used to baby-sit with him. We played with electric trains, played cowboys and also built sandcastles in his sand box. His Dad usually brought him funny books from the newsstand when he came home for lunch. We would read them and then set up a newsstand on a rock wall where mill workers passed on their way home from work. We would sell them all in just a few minutes after work. We sold them for half of what his dad paid for them.

On summer nights we gathered under the street lights to play hide and seek. There would be 10 to 12 kids playing. We would play until 10 o'clock or later. Our dad would call us in before he went to work on the graveyard shift, and after he left we would sneak back out to play some more.

Halloween found local boys hanging rocking chairs on telephone poles. A state senator who lived near us would give us cups of ice cream. The catch was—we had to go in the house to get it.

When it snowed, the streets were closed to let us sleigh ride. We could go from the school house all the way to town to the post office, under traffic lights they had turned off. It was downhill all the way. We would sneak coal from our family's coal pile and get

*Follow the arrow to the foot of the hill which is the town of Canton. The arrows show the path where we would sleigh ride. They would block off the streets on both sides to give us a clean path to town. The arrows are pointing out Academy Street.*

a big barrel and build a fire to keep us warm when we got back up to the top of the hill after sleighing down.

Back to the doctor who delivered us—well—he had a son who is about our age, maybe a year younger. He didn't know it but he was my childhood heart throb until I was in high school. He made my childhood a little more special. Everyone needs a dream. I was so disappointed when he got married to someone else. Of course, he never knew of my heartbreak—I was just a neighbor friend to him. I survived and had a happy life, however.

Wallace, my older brother, bought us our only "dy-de" doll or a wet-me-doll. In other words , it wet on itself and you had to change it's diaper. He also bought us a little wicker wooden cradle for the doll to sleep in. He really seemed proud when he gave the cradle to us. I remember him and "mom" watching to see what we would do when we got it. They seemed to get pleasure out of giving things to us. After all—we were their little twin sisters!

When he would come home from work Wallace would pick us up, one at a time, and hold us up in the air over his head. It was so much fun. Your tummy felt so weird!!! Now when I see a child being lifted I wonder what memories the child will have.

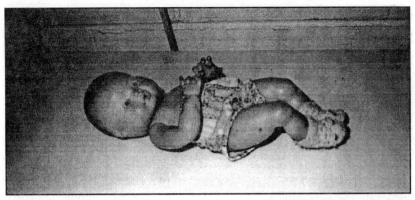

*Our Dy-Dee doll. Note the round mouth for the bottle.*

My childhood wasn't all fun and games, however, mostly because of the local bar. Almost always on his day off my dad would be up by eight o'clock and gone to town. He would stay there all day. When he came home after drinking he was usually loud and he and my mom would get into a loud verbal exchange. I just knew the whole neighborhood knew. My brothers told him if he didn't quit, the next time they would put him in the bathtub with cold water to sober him up. Well, he did and they did what they had promised. My twin and I sat upstairs in the middle of the bed

*The telephone pole in the center of the picture is where we gathered to play hide and seek. Senator J.T. Bailey's house is seen to the left of the picture behind the forked tree. Dr. Johnson's house is the big white one.*

hugging each other—scared they were going to drown him, or from the sound of it, kill him. Of course, they didn't. They got him out and dried him off and put him to bed, daring him to get up. It weaned him for a while but he still drank his beer whenever he could.

I swam a lot at the local YMCA as a child. After we swam we were always hungry. The grocery store was next door and it also had a soda fountain. We stopped to get an ice cream or something to drink. In the summer when it was hot, we got other things and charged them to our dad's account. This would run the grocery bill up. The things were charged and then the amount was taken from our dad's paycheck on payday. If it got too big he would tell them not to let us get anything. Well not to be outdone, when we went to the store for our mother for groceries, we'd get a package of cookies and as much candy as I could buy. We would have to eat the whole box before we got home because we couldn't hide it. The store clerks knew what we were doing and they would smile. Sometimes they would avoid us and not want to wait on us.

I cried a lot as a child, probably just growing pains and the fact that my mom was "old" and my dad was just a mill hand. Most of the neighborhood kids' parents were young, and only had one or two children. Our family had ten children, so the money had to stretch further. After all, the twins were the last born so my mom was up in years, or so it seemed to me. Most people living around us were professionals and made a lot more money than a mill hand like my dad. We still heated our house with coal while other houses were heated with furnaces. I hated it when I had to carry coal for the fire. It would get my hands all black.

"Buzz," my older brother, was to keep kindling for the fire in the morning. Well, one night he had something to do and didn't want to get it in. He gave an older sister money if she would cut it for him. My sister wasn't used to using the ax so when she came down with the ax it got her right between the big toe and her second toe. The blood flowed everywhere. Her toe wasn't cut off but her big toe was separated slightly from the other toes. She had been holding the wood still with her foot so she could chop it. Of course, that was the end of her helping to get the kindling and "Buzz" got chewed out for letting her do it.

*First Baptist Church of Canton in the 50s.*

# I.
# Canton

*Champion Paper and Fiber Co.*

# Twins

I was one of twin girls born in 1929, the last of ten children. I went by the nickname of "Jody" and my twin was "Tommie." Our real names were Josephine and Thomasine Paxton. When I married, my mother-in-law didn't like either the name Jody of Josephine so she shortened it to "Jo." I go by that name today, mostly because it's easy to write. My job requires my signature a lot.

We were born at home and were delivered by a neighbor doctor. We were raised in the house where we were born and it is still in the family today. We both married men with the first name of "Bill." I married Billy Furman Wood and she married Bill Harkins. They were both from Canton, N.C. We both have four children and we both lost a child. Both "Bills" served in World War II in the Navy. Both of their fathers died at a young age, leaving them to be raised by a mother left with several children.

Reasons I Liked Being a Twin
1. I had my own live-in playmate.
2. She was a good warm bedfellow on a cold night.
3. When we begged for something we usually got it, as there were two of us begging.
4. I guess I liked the attention a little, too.
5. I was hardly ever alone.
6. We were special and different.

Reasons I Didn't Like Being a Twin
1. I guess the biggest thing with me was that we didn't get invited to birthday parties sometimes. We sometimes had different friends at school. If the child was allowed to invite

*1948 Graduation. Tommie and Jody.*

     just so many children, then we would be omitted, as it would make the count too many.

2.    Didn't get to go to Virginia as a child because there wasn't enough room in the car for both of us.

3.    We only got to buy one annual at school. We had to share. One year she got to keep it and the next year I got to.

4.    Only one twin, Tommie, went to college because I felt it would be too much to send us both. My dad offered to send me to a business school in Asheville but by then I had a good job, so I didn't go.

*The twins as babies with brother Buzz and siter Winnie.*

*First cosines William Henderson and Katherine Jones, Uncle Port's Twins.*

## Twins in the family

There were two sets of twins in our family. We had twin cousins. My mom's brother and his wife were the parents of a set of twins, a boy and a girl. They were several years younger than me and Tommie. They lived in another town.

One summer there was an illness in their family and my mom brought them home to live with us, and they ended up staying all summer in Canton. Mom kept and took care of them until they went back with their parents. They were about four years old at the time. It gave us someone to play with.

*View of Canton from our upstairs window.*
*(Champion Mill is in the background)*

*The Old Locust Field Church located at the Locust Field Cemetery.*

# Champion—Town—People

Canton, North Carolina is the town I grew up in. It developed when the Champion Paper and Fiber Company located here in 1908. People built houses and stores around the plant along with a livery stable.

A school was started called the "Academy" and some of the older members of our family attended it. It was torn down when I was a child. As the town grew, there was a need for more schools. One was started on a hill in an area referred to as North Canton and the school was named "North Canton."

Below the mill an area developed known as "Fiberville." My understanding is this area was developed for the mill hands. It was on the bank of the Pigeon River and I remember a big flood in the area as a child. The people had to leave their homes and stand on a hill above it and see their homes under water below. Few houses remain there today as a road took part of the property and others have moved away.

The first church founded in Haywood County was founded in the early 1800s and was called "Locust Field." A cemetery was formed around it and is called the "Old Locust Field Cemetery." The church is gone but the spot where it stood is still maintained and an arch remains there to mark it.

On the opposite side of town from North Canton, an area developed and a new school was built and it was called "Pennsylvania Avenue". This is the school I attended. I lived right below it and could walk to school in about 3-5 minutes. A large percentage of the professional people settled in this area. It was within walking distance to their jobs. In this area lived three doctors, four dentists, two lawyers, one eye doctor, two N.C. senators, a postmaster, three pharmacists, a former N.C. governor, the funeral home and several store owners. I didn't realize until I started writing that I lived in the middle of them.

# OUR NEIGHBORS IN TOWN

*Doctors:*
Dr. W. C. Johnson
Dr. Joe Bob Westmoreland
Dr. J. R. Reeves

**Dentists:**
Dr. A. W. Bottoms
Dr. Carey T. Wells, Sr.
Dr. Carey T. Wells, Jr.
Dr. A. P. Cline
Dr. Luther Rollins

**Lawyer:**
Walter Clark, Sr.
Sam Robinson

**Eye Doctor:**
Dr. Robert K. Harpe, Sr.

**Former Governor:**
Dan Moore

**N.C. Senators:**
Senator Clyde R. Hoey
Senator J. T. Bailey

**Postmaster:**
Mr. Bell

**Fire Chief:**
Charlie Westmoreland
(father of Joe Bob)

**Personnel Manager at Champion:**
W. Lee McElrath

**Pharmacists:**
Dr. Barefoot
Dr. Burris
Dr. Hendrix
Dr. Robinson

**Preachers:**
Rev. Hammond
Preacher Mosteller

**Photographer:**

Guy Teague

*The house where I grew up in town. Our house was one of the first houses in the area. The others were built later on lots around it.*

Wells Funeral Home was in our area. Also in our area were: Mr. Morgan of the Meat Market, Mr. Nichols of the clothing store, and Mr. Winner of the clothing store. Belk-Hudson was owned by Margaret Hudson and husband, the clothing store by Mr. and Mrs. Hill, and W.G. Cole and Mr. Wycle ran Cole and Wykle's. The first elevator in town was in the Medical Building, built by some of the doctors and dentists.

Professor Charlie F. "Pop" Owen lived in a house where the First Baptist Church now stands. He was the father of three sons, who all became doctors. They were Charles, Robert, and Boyd Owen, all who practiced in Haywood County. "Pop" was the principal at Patton School and was also a preacher.

H.A. Helder, the Champion manager, also lived on Pennsylvania Avenue.

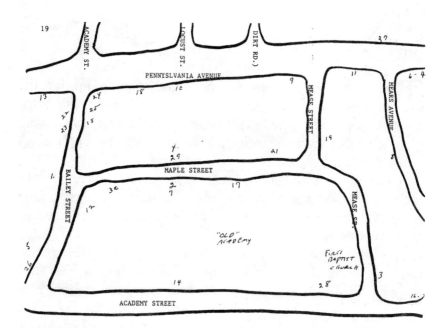

Doctors :
1 - Dr. W. C. Johnson
2 - Dr. Joe Bob Westmorland
3 - Dr. J.R. Reeves
  Dentists
4 - Dr. A.W. Bottoms.
5. DR. Carey T. Wells,Sr.
6 - Dr.A.P. Cline, SR.
7 - Dr. Luther Rollins
  Lawyer:
  8 - Walter Clark, Sr.
  Eye doctor:
9 - Dr. Robert  King Harpe, SR.
  Former governor:
10 Dan Moore
  N.C. Senator:
  1. Sen. Clyde R. Hoey
  2. Sen J.T. Bailey
  Postmaster:
13 Mr. Bell
  Fire Chief:
14 Charlie Westmoreland
  Father of Dr. Joe Bob
  Pharmists:
15 Dr. Barefoot
16 Dr. Burris
17 Dr. Hendrix

Personnel Manager:
18 W. Lee McElrath
  Photographer for the paper:
19 Guy Teague
20 Wells Funeral Home

21 Mr. Morgan owner of Morgan's meat mkt.
22 Mr. Nichols owner of NIchol's Clothing Store
23 Mr. Harry Winner owner of Winner's clothing
24 Mgt. Hudson owner of Belk-Hudson
25 Mr. and Mrs. Hill owner of Hill's variety
26 W.G. Cole and FRank Wykle co-owners of
     Cole and Wykle men's store
27 Manager of Champion Paper Co.-H.A. Helder
28 Professor"PoP" Owen principal of Patton
     school and father of  Boyd,
     Robert and Charles Owen (doctors
29. 23 Maple STreet(our house)
30.Rev. George Hammond (Preacher)

# My Very First Memories

The very first memories I have are signing up for the first grade with my mom and twin sister. I remember being downstairs in the cafeteria of Pennsylvania Avenue School with a lot of other parents with children also signing up. I don't remember the first day of school, however.

My second memory is when my twin sister and I were taken to the doctor's office for a checkup ordered by the school. I remember the doctor looking at my eyes and listening to our chest and then ordering vitamins for us to take. I also remember my mom giving us cod liver oil. How I hated the taste of it. That only goes to show that maybe there is something to fish oil being good for you. They thought that back in the 1930s. My mom used to fix eggnog for us to drink. I did all right with it until one day I got the last in the pitcher. When I got to the bottom of the glass, I saw it had clumps of raw egg in it and nearly threw up. After that, I hated those things. I won't drink eggnog today.

I remember the second grade because the teacher was so sweet. She was a little overweight and an old maid. I later became friends with her niece, who was in the same grade as me. Their parents ran a grocery store in town. There were several back then.

In fifth grade, a boy had eaten ramps the day before (Sunday) and the teacher made him sit in a chair outside the door. The odor from the ramps was so bad. That was my first introduction to ramps. I thought they were definitely to be avoided. So it seems school played a big part in my younger years as far as memory goes.

We were checked for lice in the fourth or fifth grade. The Health Department Nurse came to our school and with the teacher checked each one of us one at a time. Anyone with "nits" or eggs had to wash their hair in kerosene and then wash again with a strong soap to get the kerosene out. A new student had transferred to our school with a head of bushy black hair. Well, it seems me and Tommie had played on the swings outside at recess with her.

There was a substitute teacher there that day and I didn't like her. She catered to the "richer" kids. I guess you would call her a social climber. She checked my head and I knew before she said it that she would say that I had "nits" so I would have to wash my hair in kerosene. The nurse never looked at my head, she just took that teacher's word for it. Us being twins, we both had to wash our hair. My Mom was fit to be tied. Guess who got to wash their heads in kerosene??? You are right!!! Me and Tommie. To make matters worse we had to carry a can to town and buy the kerosene. If you have never carried it before, I'll tell you it spills real easy and penetrates what it touches. It is hard to get out of your clothes. Did it ever burn our head!!! Was I humiliated??? Yes! To this day I can't think any good thought about that teacher.

Another time we were playing with a girl some game where you have to sit on the ground. She was visiting in the neighborhood with her granny, I guess. Anyway she didn't live in the area. When she bent over I couldn't believe what I saw. She had "red lice" crawling everywhere in her hair. I didn't play with her anymore as I didn't want the kerosene treatment again. I made myself believe that the red ones had come off of a rose bush because that's what they look like. You may gather that lice was a problem back then. Children are still checked today by a Health Nurse each year.

There were also a lot of cockroaches. The town women thought they were brought home in their husband's lunch boxes from the paper mill. At night after dark if you turned on the light in the downstairs dining room, they would run everywhere to hide. Some of them were pretty big, with long antenna-like appendages. They were only in that one room. Then they just mysteriously quit being there.

# Unusual Noises

The house on Maple Street where I grew up had unusual noises. As kids like to scare others, they would make the noises out to be more than they were. When we came home from school and everyone was gone and the house was empty, we did not stay in the house long. We went in long enough to discover no one there, put our books down and go back outside. We began to wish someone would hurry and come home so we wouldn't be alone. The house would be so quiet, it was eerie. The least sound we heard, if we stayed in the house would send us right back outside. This was in the summer or winter. The noises were no more than the wind making a two-story house creak or maybe a mouse running in between the walls or under the floor. Since we didn't have *De-Con* to poison them or a cat to catch them, almost everyone had a few mice. I still stop and listen when I hear a sound in the house when I visit there. Of course, I never hear any now. I think it was just too many scary movies I went to as a child. They made our imagination run away with us.

# Dark Hole

Our house in town was two stories with an attic and a dirt basement. Our parents slept downstairs and the children slept upstairs. There were three bedrooms upstairs—and in the bigger bedroom was the door leading to the attic.

It was a small door and in the corner of the room. We were always told that it was the "dark hole" and something would get us if we went in there. They must have been pretty convincing because none of the children—to my knowledge—ever ventured near it. We would get so far and then chicken out. Well, it convinced me

*The small door in the corner of the room...The Dark Hole!*

to the point that I don't even like to look in there today. It really was just an unfinished attic room without any flooring. The electric wiring was exposed and if you didn't walk right on the rafters you could get on that wiring and maybe get hurt bad. Even the grandchildren wouldn't go near that door, even though it was never locked. We thought the "boogy man" was in there.

After going to a spooky movie our imagination could run away with us. We thought—like in the movies—that hands would come out of the door while we slept and smother us in our sleep. We never put our bed near the door.

One time our brother, Buzz, put his bed there just to show us that there was no harm in it. Sure enough, nothing happened to him. There were usually two beds in the room by the attic with children sleeping in them. After all, there were ten children in the family. I finally looked into the attic after I was grown and sure enough it was just a dusty old attic with cob webs and probably spiders. I'm sure a few mice played there too. So reason enough for us to stay out. Seems like someone mentioned that maybe Santa Claus was there sometime. No matter the reason—we didn't disobey when told to say away from it.

# Deliveries

Our local paper mill also owned a grocery store. The employees of the mill would charge their groceries and the cost would be taken from their paycheck every two weeks on payday. They delivered groceries to our door by the Champion Employees Store truck. You just called in your order and they made their rounds every day and brought them to your door.

Our milk was also delivered by truck. Every other day we put our empty cleaned glass bottles on the porch and they would be replaced with full bottles of milk. Pretty neat!!! It sure was easier than when I moved to the country and had to go get the cows and then milk them for our milk. Sometimes the cows would be way off in the woods and we would have to find them and bring them home to the barn. However, it did come in handy during a long snowy spell. We'd see people all bundled up with scarves, hats and

*Glass quart and pint milk bottles.*

overshoes walking to the store about a mile and one half away. We'd be cozy warm in our house by a cozy fire.

We used milk to make our bread. You've never tasted any better biscuits and corn-bread than those that were made with good rich whole cow milk. We always kept apples for fresh applesauce that we always ate with pork. It's supposed to help with the digestion of pork, according to old timers.

# Accidents

Mom had the kitchen stove "hot" one day cooking supper. She used coal to cook with. Well, the kettle got to boiling pretty "big" so she took it off and set it in the wood box that sat by the stove. The box was for kindling to start the fire.

Being a nosy kid, I climbed upon the side of the wood box to see what was cooking. My foot slipped and into the kettle it went —right into the scalding water. Did I ever yell!! Did it ever hurt!! I cried and screamed until my dad got home. Mom tried to quieten me and made me lay down on the bed. It didn't work as I still cried because it burned so. My dad had been to the grocery store. He gave me a box of saltine crackers that he said I could have all to

*The kettle my foot slipped into.*

myself, if I would quit crying. It worked as I was about cried out anyway. I was probably hungry, which is why I was looking to see what was cooking.

My sister, Winnie, made some candy one day when our parents were gone. Well, an older sister felt like she was in charge and told Winnie she shouldn't have made the candy. This was during the time of sugar rationing. They got into an argument about it.

The candy had just been taken off of the stove and was scalding hot. They started running through the house with one right behind the other. The one in the front went through the door and then slammed it shut behind her to try to stop the other one from chasing her. Well, the door slammed right up against that pot of candy and spilled it all over Winnie's arm. It burned her from the elbow to the hand. Well, she screamed and cried. If you have ever been splattered by hot candy—you know how it burns. It hurts like crazy and is almost impossible to get off of the skin. This makes it burn a long time. I don't remember what she got for a consolation prize.

The same sister, Winnie, went to visit a playmate and they climbed up on a fence. Well, Winnie slipped and fell on the barbed wire and cut an eight- to ten-inch gash on the back of her thigh. It was gapping open and looked terrible. It had to have stitches. I remember her being brought home with someone carrying her in their arms and blood was everywhere.

*Steps and wall where "Black Friends" waited to ask for the "lights."*

# Lights

The black community in Canton was divided into two different areas. One is the area near the Morning Star school and the other area was behind the Penn Avenue school.

The area of our community sloped and faced the Champion plant. On the back side of the hill was where a small group of black people lived. Our father usually raised two pigs and slaughtered them in the fall when the weather turned cold. Each year someone from the black community would come and stand at the foot of the steps and wait for someone to come out. When they did they would ask for the "lights" of the pigs. They would say "you gave them to so and so last year, can we have them this year?" We usually discarded this part of the pig but they did something with them. They were always respectful and polite and never came close to the house. They would wait for us to bring the "lights" out to them.

# Red Devil Lye

While staying with my mother at my grandparents while my grandmother was sick one summer, we went to a funeral for a small child. I remember standing at the grave and seeing the little baby in the casket.

There were "purple splotches" all over its body where the Red Devil Lye had eaten through the body to the outside. Its mother had mixed the Red Devil Lye in a glass with water and had sat it on the table and turned her back to do something. While her back was turned the baby got it and drank it. The mixture looked like a glass of milk as it was white when mixed. The mother was going to use it in her washing machine.

At the grave the mother was screaming "I can't go home without my baby!" It was rather traumatic to us as we were just children ourselves. We had gone with a cousin to the funeral.

# Softball Games

When I was a child our little town was full of activity. The mill was there and you either worked in it or you were involved in something supporting it. There were a lot of mill hands and they formed a softball team.

We lived close to town and the games were within walking distance. There were lots of kids to play with and things to do. At night in the summer my dad and his brother played on the local softball team. My uncle played more than my dad. My dad had one leg shorter than the other as the result of an accident in the mill that left the leg, when healed, shorter than the other leg. My uncle stood about six feet tall and was very stout. My dad was shorter and could not run as fast because of his short leg.

My mother took us twins to the games when they played. We were small, about 5 or 6 years old. We would play in the grass by the ballfield until it got dark. Then we would sit with our mother on the benches. The longer we sat the harder the benches got. We also got cold after the sun went down, as the ballfield was close to the river. She wouldn't let us go home even though we lived just up the street. She made us stay with her.

I would get so sleepy I thought I would die for sure. I would lay my head on her lap for awhile—then I would sit up—I was totally miserable. I'd beg her to go home but she wouldn't leave until the game was over. I'll never forget how miserable I felt and how sleepy I was. When I see a sleepy child now I can relate to it.

# Fish Pond

My mom was forever wanting to improve our place. She decided she wanted a fish pond. Now this was a round pond with a rim on it where you could sit on it if you wanted to. A rock mason build it to her specifications. It was built in the back yard

*It used to look like this with lily pads.*

behind the house. She got some goldfish and put them in the pond. She also got lily pads so frogs could sit on them.

A couple of years went by and then one summer my brother, Buzz, and some of his friends went to the Pigeon River fishing and to get whatever else they could catch. They brought home a snake, a turtle and some fish that were still alive. They put them in the pond. They didn't stop to think what

*The fish pond as it looks today.*

these fish, snake, and turtle would do to the goldfish. Mom started missing them a day at a time. When she got to talking about it—someone told her about the things the boys had put in the pond. She was made at those boys!!! She made them drain the pond and get their things out. They had eaten all of her goldfish. They refilled the pond with water but no more goldfish were put in it.

Every spring that pond had to be cleaned out. It didn't have a drain so the water had to be dipped out a bucket at a time. It would take all day to clean it. It is filled with dirt today and flowers get planted in it at times.

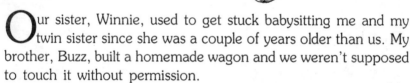

# Wagon

Our sister, Winnie, used to get stuck babysitting me and my twin sister since she was a couple of years older than us. My brother, Buzz, built a homemade wagon and we weren't supposed to touch it without permission.

One day my mother was gone and Winnie was watching us. Buzz, who owned the wagon, was also out mowing yards and wasn't at home. Well, me and Tommie convinced Winnie that it was all right to ride the wagon. We pulled it to the top of the hill and down we went.

Tommie was guiding it and Winnie was sitting behind her. I was standing up on the back as there was no place for me to sit down. When we got to the bottom of the hill, the wagon was slowing down almost to a standstill. I jumped off to push so it would keep rolling. My foot slipped and it got lodged between the wheel and the wagon bed. I was screaming to stop the wagon—no pain—I just couldn't keep up. After we got it stopped, we discovered my heel was coated in axle grease and definitely was cut as we could see the gash. Still no pain.

*Left: Winnie with the twins, Tommy and Jody. Top right: Bailey street. At the bottom of the hill is where I jumped off and caught my heel. Bottom right: Imagine me sitting on the edge of the bathtub with my foot over the wash basin and me trying to faint into the bathtub backwards, all the while Winnie is trying to get the grease off my heel.*

Winnie was beside herself. First, we shouldn't have had the wagon out and—then I get hurt—boy was she in trouble!!! We put the wagon up as best we could. There was no blood on it because of so much grease—which was to our advantage. The next step was to get the grease off of my foot before anyone came home. Our bathtub sat along side the wash basin. Winnie had me sitting on the side of the tub rim and putting my foot in the wash basin. As she washed my foot she was rubbing it trying to get the grease off of it and I began to get weak and felt like I was going to pass out. I was going backward into the tub. She said to me "for heaven's sake, it's not bad enough, you get hurt, now you're trying to faint on me too!!! She put cold water on my face to bring me to. We successfully kept this from anyone but I bet Winnie didn't forget and wasn't eager to baby-sit again.

# Recreation Park

One year the Champion Paper Mill rewarded the mill employees with a company paid picnic at the Asheville Recreation Park. Each employee got two tickets. We were taken over on a bus they provided. Our mom and Wallace, our older brother, took us. Mom and one of the twins used Daddy's two tickets and the other twin shared Wallace's tickets. Each employee was given so many tickets to each attraction.

They had a big time riding us twins on the rides. We were just little girls then. I can see Mama and Wallace now talking among themselves about the tickets. At lunch the mill provided hot dogs and drinks we got with food tickets. It was very well organized. We rode the ferris wheel with our mom. The ferris wheel was enclosed with screen wire with doors that closed after you got in and were seated. The seats faced each other and we didn't necessarily have to be strapped in but of course we had to. It could carry four to six people, according to the size of them. We could even stand up while it was going around. Our mom insisted we stay seated. It was a wonderful day. I don't remember how many of these picnics there were, as I only remember the one.

# Money Tree

As children, me and Tommie were rarely in the house. We went outside unless it was raining or too cold. I really don't believe it ever got too cold, as we stayed out most of the time.

There was an apple tree that stood above the garden between our neighbor's house and ours. It had perfect limbs for a good swing. We played under that tree a lot.

To the left of the tree was a little building that my dad would sleep in during the day when he was working the night shift. There was too much noise in the house with the kids home from school.

One day before the garden was planted, Tommie and I got a wild notion to grow something. We decided to grow some money trees. We went to the house and got our pennies. We always had pennies. We proceeded to plant a row of our pennies. We were very sincere about it.

I don't know whose idea it was and she reminded me of this story, so I kind of think maybe it was her idea. When we went in the house for supper everyone was watching us. Someone said "so you are going to grow a money tree??"

Tommie said that she remembers all eyes were on us and there was a twinkle in their eyes, as though they were trying to keep from laughing. Of course, we got no money tree but I think it was a good idea, had it worked.

# Cows

We lived in town but town ordinances allowed a cow to be inside the city limits. Our barn was to the left of the house. In the daytime the cow stayed in a neighbor's pasture. The pasture belonged to Charlie Owen and we rented pasture from him. The pasture was located where the First Baptist Church in Canton is located now.

At night the cow was brought into the barn by my two oldest brothers. It took them both because the cow would not cooperate at all. She hated to be tied and she would show her displeasure by running this way and that and rearing up on her hind legs and kicking her front legs at you. I was terrified that she would hurt my brothers or get away and hurt me. I'd watch from the window in the house until she was safely in the barn with the door locked and my brothers were in the house. As long as the cow was pastured in Mr. Owen's lot, this was the routine every night and I was glad when she was moved to another pasture.

One day I went to the barn and climbed into the corn crib. The cow was in the barn stall eating her feed. I peeped through the boards looking at her and thinking how brave I was to be there that close to her. All of a sudden she raised her head and looked straight at me through the cracks of the boards with her two big brown eyes. It scared me so I was in a trance for a minute, then I jumped down from that corn crib and ran home as fast as I could—all the time seeing those big brown eyes.

After the town ordinance was changed restricting cattle from inside the city limits, my parents bought a piece of land for her to stay in that was outside the city limits. The land was laid out like a "V." It went down to the bottom and then back up on the other side (like a dip). At the foot of the hill we had a pigpen. I was to take feed to the pigs while my mom milked. I also had some corn shucks from corn to take to the pigs. Well, down the hill I went but the cow liked what I had better than what was offered her while my mom tried to milk her. So, she proceeded to come to see what I had. They were in a bag but one of the shucks was sticking out and the cow could see it. Of course, she had to run and kick up her heels (right at me). I ran to the bottom of the hill with corn shucks trailing behind. At last she stopped to eat them and leave me alone. So much for the milking.

There were always apples to gather at this pasture in the fall. The trees were on the hill so of course we had to chase the apples when they fell off the tree. We had to stay a step ahead of the cow, as she liked apples too. Daddy would shake the trees and we would to scramble to get the apples. I hated to gather those apples. I would stay close to the fence and dart out every now and then when the cow wasn't looking and back to the fence I would go. I was terrified of that cow chasing me.

# Child Games

As a family we got along very well. The older children would play games with the younger ones. We played "mumbly peg" sitting on the front lawn with our brother and sister, Buzz and Winnie. We'd flip the knife to see how it would land. The blade had to stick up in the ground for you to win. You stuck one blade in the ground and one stuck straight out. You took hold of the smooth end of the knife and flipped it up slightly in the air. We passed a lot of time playing this. We also played "Jacks"—where

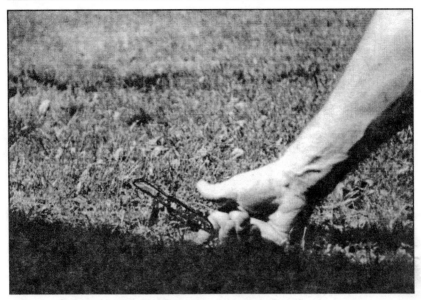

*A knife in position to flip while playing Mumbley Peg.*

we threw a small rubber ball up in the air and then tried to pick up as many jacks as you could before you caught the ball. "Jacks" were made of metal with soft rounded ends so they wouldn't hurt you. On cold nights in the winter we would play Monopoly in the living room until late and even continue the next day as we never finished a game.

In front of our house were a set of concrete steps, about twelve in number. My brother, Buzz, fell down them when he was very young and broke his leg. After it healed he walked with a slight limp. We also used chalk to mark off a "Hop Scotch" on the pavement. We would hop through it for hours. We threw a rock and we hopped to the square it was in and we had to hop over that one. We had to turn around and go back picking up the rock as we went by the block it was in.

We also played with neighborhood children on a grapevine swing that hung out over the road. We would take turns swinging out over the road where cars run. Luckily, a car never came by while we were swinging. I would be terrified if I saw children doing that today. We always found something to do outside, and didn't ever get in trouble. We never stayed inside unless it was to eat or sleep or in school.

# Revival

In the summer we usually had a least two "tent meetings" in our town. One was set up right next to the movie theater. My Mom took me and my twin, Tommie, every night it was there. She would always sit up front, but we kids would sit on the back row. We behaved because if we didn't we would hear about it later.

One night a friend of ours was sitting with us. About half way through the service she slipped something in our hand and told us to chew it real good. At this point I was getting bored so this was a good diversion. I thought it was candy. Well—we chewed it real good like she said and then our tongue and mouth started burning. She had given us "hot pepper". Our mouths burned until preaching was over. We had to sit there and "take it" as we weren't' allowed to leave the service. She thought it was funny and she laughed and laughed. They had to ask her to be quiet. The preacher got louder and louder preaching. He'd wipe sweat from his face and keep right on preaching. He'd prance across the front of the building until I was afraid he would have a heart attack. We didn't mind going to these meetings because we liked to see the preacher get "carried away".

One tent meeting when we were younger, our Mom used to come and sit with us when the preacher and the congregation started shouting. She thought it would scare us, which it did! They would get up on the benches and walk from one to the other and we watched to see if they were going to fall as they weren't looking where they were stepping, they were so busy shouting.

My Mom was very religious and went to church a lot. She even went to the Negro church in our area. They treated her like royalty. They always called her name out as a visitor. I never went to a "black" church with her. Not that I didn't want to, she didn't ever take me. I do remember visiting in one of the Negro homes with my Mom. They were always clean and they were always nice to us.

# Christmas

My most vivid Christmas was when my brother and sisters tried to put me and Tommie to bed for Santa Claus to come. They covered us up but we didn't want to say in bed, so they stayed with us. They kept telling us, "there's a noise on the roof top. I bet it's Santa Claus waiting for you to go to sleep. Close your eyes so he will think you're asleep." Of course, we were so excited there just wasn't any going to sleep.

After a bit they said that Santa Claus had come so we could get up and come downstairs. They were more excited than we were. That year must have been a lean year because we both got a red dump truck and no doll!! I was a little disappointed as I didn't see anyone else with gifts. I wondered to myself, "where are the rest of the gifts?" The other children were really too old to be getting Santa Claus gifts anyway. We wore those trucks out hauling dirt on the bank by our house.

This is about the same time we were playing with the doctor's son that lived across the street from us. So I guess there was an ulterior motive for us getting a boy's toy. He also had a sand box which we played in.

# Christmas Gifts

One Christmas day my sisters took me and Tommie Christmas shopping on Christmas eve. We went to the dime store because we were each given a dime to buy gifts for everyone. Winnie took Tommie, and Dee took me and we separated when we got to the store, with them going to one side of the store and us to the other. We shopped about an hour, looking everything over. I finally found what I wanted to buy. I picked out a set of glass crystal cut salt and pepper shakers that set on a glass tray. They cost a nickel. They were for my parents together. We paid for them and continued to shop. This way we saved a penny as we didn't have to pay tax until it was a dime. We decided on combs for the other gifts at a penny each.

When we got home we discovered we had both bought identical salt and pepper shakers. We gave them to our parents anyway as the stores were closed and the next day was Christmas. Their thinking was if one gets broken, there would be a replacement. They thought it was "cute" that we had picked out the same thing.

# Dentist

Since we lived so close to town, we walked everywhere we went. We were allowed to go to the dentist alone. I remember one time I went alone one morning. I think I had a tooth pulled. He filled another tooth before he pulled the tooth, however. So I was there for some time. After he pulled the tooth he told me that I needed another appointment and to make it before I left. So I go to the front desk to tell the girl to make it. I was about twelve or thirteen at the time.

Well, I got dizzy as could be as I stood there. I felt like I was going to faint as I had fainted before and knew how I felt. She looked up at me and said "are you all right?" I said, "no, I feel a little dizzy." She answered by saying that I was as white as a sheet and I should sit down. She called for the dentist but when he got there, I had already went to the floor.

When I came to, I wanted to go home but they made me go and lay down on a cot they had in one of the rooms. They put cold cloths to my face and covered me up with a blanket. They wanted to call my Mom but I talked them out of it by telling them she wasn't home. I stayed there well over an hour before they would let me up. I still felt a little weak and dizzy.

When I finally went home my Mom wanted to know where I had been so long. I said "at the dentist" and hoped she wouldn't question me any further. She was busy and didn't notice me very much. I never did tell anyone about it and evidently the dentist didn't call and tell anyone as it was never mentioned.

# Whipping

One day Tommie slipped off and went to play at a neighbor's house. She had been gone several hours. My mother told me to go and get her and get back home or we would both get a spanking. Since we had never had a spanking I didn't believe her. When I got there, they were at the garden near their barn. They were putting corn stalks over the fence for the cows to eat. So—I go down to check it out. Well—it looked pretty interesting so I didn't get into going back home right away.

After another hour or so we went home. Our Mom met us with a "keen hickory." That was the first and only whipping we ever got. I guess it weaned us. It made "red" stripes on our legs and back. Did it ever burn and hurt!! Tommie got into the bath tub with cold water to make hers quit hurting. It was still red the next day. That's the only time I remember getting whipped. We were usually good kids.

# Fireplace

One winter our Dad decided to use the fireplace in the living room for our heat for the winter. What a mistake!! We liked to have froze. It was small and only about two people, definitely no more than three, could stand in front of it at a time. We fought over who got to stand there sometimes. We had chairs in front of it but it was cold sitting in them. Which ever side of your body faced the "fire" was what kept warm. Our legs would "cook" and turned deep purple or "pyiety". We used to refer to this as the blood being cooked in our legs.

You can guess by now that we went to bed early. No TV and little radio unless it was Saturday night. Then we would listen to the Grand Ole Opry. I went to sleep many a Saturday night listening to the "Opry". I am sure thousands of other people did the same thing.

Our only other heat was in the kitchen from the coal fired cook stove. Sometimes the coal would be "no good" and it wouldn't burn. Then the house would be cold. You couldn't tell by looking at coal if it would burn or not. It could be as hard as a rock and would not burn at all. It would have to be taken out and replaced with another piece. You better believe it—the next winter we had better heat.

# Paper Man

Our daily paper was delivered to our house just as it is now. It was a rare occasion when we didn't get one. The man who delivered it was well known in town. He had a covered shed he always set up on Main Street on payday right across from the bank. He would get you as you came out of the bank after cashing your check from the mill. If he missed you there, he would see you on the street the next week. He always carried his accounting book and he didn't mind to ask you for the paper money. Everybody paid this way as he never sent out bills. If you didn't pay after a time he would just stop your paper.

He delivered the paper for many years. He attended all the ball games in Canton whether they be softball or football. He was a big supporter of sports.

# Snow Of '36

What a beautiful sight to wake up to a big snow as a child. It would always be so still you knew what had taken place while you slept. When a child of seven—one such morning occurred—with the windows and doors half covered with snow. You barely could open the doors because of the weight of the snow against them. It stayed cold so long, for over a week, that the snow froze solid.

My Dad dug a tunnel walkway to his job at Champion. He dug the tunnel to the foot of the hill by the church and from there the streets were in better shape. He didn't miss time from work because of the snow. The tunnel he dug was so deep you could barely see the top of his head when he walked through it. It was frozen so hard that I could sit on it like I was on a rock wall. I could swing my legs out and not touch the ground. We also cut out squares of frozen snow and made an Eskimo igloo. We dared not go in it, however.

When I was about six I remember being taken to school by my Mom and it would be snowing so hard you could barely see your way. We were bundled up like Eskimos. She would hold our hands with a twin at each side. I was in the first grade at school and she would come and get us after school to get us home safely.

If you were lucky you had rubber overshoes. Being not so luc.
and with my Dad supporting eight children, I had to wear big sock.
over my shoes to keep the snow out. We took them off when we got
to school and put them on a radiator to dry. The halls were filled with
hanging wet socks. We weren't the only ones without overshoes.
Remember, this was the Depression.

We had lots of snow when I was growing up. The town would block
off the street that went downhill, for us to sleigh ride on. One place
we could ride from the top of the hill at the schoolhouse all the way
into town to the front of the Post Office. The streets were impassable
anyway. We would sleigh until our clothes got cold and wet and then
we would go in and change to dry ones. We would get warmed up
and off we would go again. We would stay out all day. We even
sleighed at night. We never got sick from it. There was always a pile
of wet clothes during a snow. We would use socks for gloves when
our mittens or gloves got wet. We also made snow cream from fresh
fallen snow. We used milk, sugar, vanilla and snow mixed together
in a bowl like cereal.

RECIPES
### Snow Cream
    4 cups of white new fallen snow (Not over a day old)
    1 cup of milk or cream
    2 tablespoonfuls of sugar
    1 teaspoon of vanilla flavoring
    Dash of salt
    Mix above ingredients and eat immediately.

### Peanut Butter Fudge
    2 cups granulated white sugar
    2 tablespoonfuls of corn syrup (white or brown)
    2 tablespoonful of margarine
    Dash of salt
    1 cup of milk
Combine in a sauce pan or a frying pan, preferably, and cook
about 5 minutes of until it gets to looking pretty syrupy, stirring it as
it cooks. Test by dropping a small amount of the candy in a little cold
water in a cup. If it hardens in the water it is ready to take off of the

stove. Add ¾ cup of either plain or crunchy peanut butter. Stir until it starts to get firm and then pour into a dish plate or platter sprayed with Pam or butter so it won't stick. Let it cool and then enjoy after slicing into squares.

### Chocolate Fudge

Make as for Peanut Butter Fudge except add 2 Tablespoons of powdered cocoa to the pan and cook as above. Omit the peanut butter unless you want peanut butter chocolate fudge.

**Eat and enjoy**.

# Measles And Chicken Pox

I was the first of the twins to get the chicken pox. My Mom had said it was all right to stay up as long as I stayed in the house. Well, everyone was out skating and I couldn't stand it any longer so on goes my coat and out I go. When my Mom found out I was outside I was promptly brought back in the house and put to bed. I stayed in a dark room which seemed like forever. It was more like ten days.

Then my twin gets them and she's bedded down with me. The door was only opened long enough to bring in food and something to drink and a warning not to pick at the sores or I would have scars. Well, we did anyway—they itched so—and off came the big scabs and it did hurt to touch those open places. And she was right—it left scars and I have a beauty on my side to prove it.

I also had the three day measles that no one to this day knows about but me. I wasn't about to spend any more time in a dark room. It was in the early summer when I first noticed them breaking out. I wore a long sleeve shirt, long pants and high rubber boots and a scarf on my head pulled down around my face. The neighbors would ask why I had those "hot" clothes on, I would say I was O.K., that I just wanted to wear them. They didn't know I was burning up but I didn't want to be put in that room again. It was the beginning of the summer vacation and I didn't want to miss anything that was going on. I even went to "Sunbeams" with that rig on. "Sunbeams" was an organization for the young people at the church. After three days the measles were gone. I also had the "Red" measles or the bad measles later. To bed for them, though, as I ran a fever and was really sick.

# Brownies

**M**y sister, Annie Dee, helped organize the first Brownie Troop in our town with a local dentist's wife assisting her. Of course, the twins had to join. They planned a coronation service to be held near the river where we could have a campfire.

We were going early enough to eat supper so we had to pack a lunch. Well, Tommie was opening a can of lunch meat to make a sandwich and the metal lid slipped and cut the fingers on her hand pretty bad. They were bleeding so bad it was dripping on to the floor. Well, seeing the blood made her kind of weak in the knees and she turned pasty white. My Mom made her lay down on the couch. One of my sisters walked in on the scene and became weak-kneed and passed out on the floor. Then here I come in and seeing me, my Mom yelled, "Get out of here! I can't handle anyone else fainting! This is enough!"

We got to the picnic with Tommie's fingers bandaged up. We had our candlelight service as planned at the river. We also got to march in the Labor Day parade as Brownies. It was cool as long as we were walking but when we stopped we were burning up.

# Patsy

**A** girl friend of my older brother, Wallace, gave him a cocker spaniel dog we named "Patsy". She was a beautiful "red" curly fluff of a dog. My brother was my Mom's favorite child, so of course, the dog had the run of the place. She was a clean good-natured dog.

My twin sister and I slept together in an upstairs bedroom over the kitchen. We would hear our Mom say—"Go get them up, Patsy!!" We knew what that meant!! She came up the stairs two at a time and would jump right in the bed—"ga-plop"—with us and start licking our faces. We learned to cover our heads when we heard the wake-up call.

My Mom used to breed cocker-spaniels and sell them. A neighbor had a black one and they would put the dogs in the basement for a couple of weeks. We weren't allowed to go near the basement during that time. The owner of the other dog got his pick of the litter and my Mom sold the other ones. "Patsy" lived to a ripe old "dog" age.

# Lye Soap

My Mom saved all grease from cooking until she got enough to make a run of lye soap. She cooked or boiled it over an outside fire in a big cast iron pot. She would start early in the morning and it would take nearly all day. She wouldn't let us near the pot as she was afraid we would get burned. She was very protective of the twins. After it cooked the desired amount of time she would pour it into a square pan and then it would harden until it was of slicing consistency. She would slice it in about three by five inch cakes about the size of soap bars today.

She used the soap on really "hard to get clean" clothes. I couldn't understand how soap made with grease could get out dirt and grease. It looked like to me it would just put it back in.

Remember the soap called "Octagen Soap"? It was good to wash your hair with. It would make it shine and manageable. I wouldn't want to use it every day as it would be too harsh.

# Spring Cleaning

Every spring my Mom broke down all the beds and took them to the back yard and scalded them with hot water. The beds and frames were all metal. After washing them she would leave them in the sun to dry. The cover over the mattress was also changed or taken off and washed. It was made of navy blue striped "pillow ticking". The pillows were covered with this also. The pillows were filled with either duck feathers or chicken feathers. These were plucked from chickens we raised at home. The feathers were taken out of the case and put in a pillow case while the "ticking" was washed and dried. Me or Tommie had to hold the case so she could put the feathers back in it. The beds always smelled so good that night when we went to bed. The quilts were sunned all day also.

I had two of these pillows and I made my children each a small one from the feathers. I just made the pillows smaller. The feathers are at least 50- years old but were still in good shape. A little flat, maybe, but still made a good pillow.

Talking about quilts, my Mom took up quilting in a big way after we all left home. She left at least thirty quilts for us. There were at least thirty or more quilt tops that hadn't been quilted. I had six of them quilted for my children and myself. The others just "got away from us".

# Snaggled Tooth

I had already lost my first front tooth when I noticed the other front tooth was loose. I "worked" it back and forth with my tongue. I never really knew why. It was just there in my mouth moving back and forth so, of course, my tongue being handy, I just kept wiggling the tooth.

One day I said to my mom, "Look, I've got another loose tooth." She told me to open my mouth and let her see, of which I did willingly.

I was so proud. I started to close my mouth when she said "wait a minute—there's something black on your tooth. Let me get it off." She started out easy and then she got firm with her fingers on the tooth and the next thing I knew she'd pulled it out.

I was disappointed as I was really enjoying it being there. It made that hole in the front of my mouth feel bigger and it looked awful with the tooth gone. Of course, I got called 'snaggled tooth."

# Blackout Drills

During World War II we had practice blackout drills. They were monitored by volunteers from the town. The siren would go off, which sounded scary and eerie to us. During a drill we were required to turn off the lights and not strike a match or turn on even a flashlight until the siren sounded an "all clear". The shades were pulled and no light whatsoever was allowed. We were told to pretend an enemy plane was overhead and if they saw your light you might be bombed as it would show them where you were . This encouraged us to obey the rules.

Our Dad was a volunteer and we usually knew when there was going to be a drill because he was usually home at night. When he left with his flashlight we knew something was up.

The lights had to stay off about 20 minutes. We kids would sit quietly and listen. Boy, was it dark!! I would go upstairs until the all clear so I could look out real quick and see the town still dark. It was pitch black as the street lights were also turned off. Even the Champion Mill had to turn off their lights and work would have to be done in the dark or not at all. If someone had a light on, a volunteer would knock on your door and tell you to turn them off. You couldn't even strike a match for a cigarette. The volunteers were allowed to carry a flashlight to get around with in case of an emergency. The "blackout drills" were a big deal to us children especially since we saw a lot of war movies.

# City Bus

As the result of World War II, transportation was hard to come by—there were few cars. If we wanted to go to Waynesville or Asheville, we caught a Trailways bus or we went by train. If it was somewhere around town we caught the city bus. The city bus went to West Canton, North Canton, Smathers Hill or North Hominy. It ran every few hours. The bus stop was in front of the Sluder Furniture store that was across the street from the post office. It would pick you up there but you sometimes would have to walk some distance to where you were going after you got off of the bus. I remember going with my Mom several times to Balsam on the train to my grandparents house.

# Balsam – Trains

As I said before, few people drove cars, because of the war causing gas for cars to be in short supply and metal for cars was also scarce. If we traveled, we walked or took the train. Since my Mother's parents lived in Balsam, we took the train most of the time since it stopped on the hill above their house. There was a bus but you had to walk a long way from the highway.

We would stand at the train station in downtown Canton and wait for it to come by. It made a big racket when it stopped—blowing steam and screeching on the rails. It also got hot when it stopped with the steam from the engine coming out from under it. My Mom would make us hold her hand and not stand too close to the tracks. She was afraid it would knock us off balance and "suck" us under the train. It did seem a little scary when it came in. We always got a seat by the window if we could.

One night we got to Grandma's after dark. We had to walk a good distance to her house. The road was dirt and there were lots of trees on both sides of the road and there were few houses. We heard all kind of noises—owls, crickets, and eerie sounds from the dark woods. It was "pitch black" because there were no street

*The Balsam Depot where we got off of the train.*

*The road we had to walk to get to our grandparents.*

lights and no moon yet evident to light the way. We held our Mom's hand and that's one time I didn't complain about having to hold her hand. That hand showed that at least they cared about me and my safety.

Our grandparent's house sat close to the road and a small creek ran in front of it. We had to cross a little bridge to get to the porch. We could sit on the front porch and watch it while we rocked in a rocking chair.

We got to go to the spring for water as there was not water in the house. There were red lizards there and the water was so cold and clear. We drank from a dipper made from a gourd. They also kept guineas that were a form of fowl or chicken. They roosted in an open shed with rods for them to sit on at night. I guess there were fifty of them. They made the most unusual sound early in the morning—and it would wake us up. One would start and the rest would follow making this sound.

A cousin of ours lived up the road from our grandparents and we played with her. We climbed trees, played in the creek and just had a big time.

*The house of our Grandparents (Jones) at Balsam. Note the bridge you had to cross to get to the house with the water in the branch below it. There was a porch there then and we would set in rocking chairs and listen to the water late in the evening and listen to the crickets chirping.*

We always attended church at the country church with our Granddad and our cousin. He sometimes had to do the preaching if the preacher was out. He was also the Sunday School Superintendent.

# Labor Day

On Labor Day our Dad was up early, at least by seven o'clock. He would call us to get up or we would miss the parade. It always started at ten o'clock but he always had us up way before that.

He was always excited for us as the rides were always in town. I am referring to the carnival rides that consisted of a merry-go-around and the ferris wheel and several others. He got to ride on a float provided for the "Old Timers" after they retired. I was in the parade once with the Brownie Scouts. It was fun. It was cool when you were walking but when you stopped, you were sweating as if you had run a race.

We would go home after the parade to eat dinner from the food left on the table for us. There was usually potato salad in the refrigerator and banana pudding on the table, among other things.

My Mom would go to the celebration and stay all day until night. She would come home long enough to eat and see if we had eaten and back she would go to listen to the singing. They met old friends they hadn't seen probably since last Labor Day.

Me and Tommie usually went to the movies after lunch. It helped to stretch our money out and kill time. During intermission we would get up and go look out the window to across the street where the rides and the celebration was taking place. They were always in town near the theater and bus stop.

A shower of rain would always come on Labor Day afternoon. Then the sun would come back out. The street would be wet when we looked out and we were glad we were in the theater when it had rained. We would stay there until four or five o'clock.

We rather ride the rides at night when the lights were on. It seemed to be more exciting. After supper we would go back to the rides and stay until about 9 o'clock. We always had to go to school the next morning. That's when school started for the new year. The first football game was on Friday after school started on Tuesday. That signaled the end of warm weather and summer. We got out our fall clothes then. Everyone would be sun-burned the first day of school after being out celebrating all day on Monday. Labor Day was a big thing to us back then. Every one came to town even if they hadn't been there since last year.

# Dreams

As a girl growing up I used to dream a lot. As a fact, for a while it was every night. I bought myself a "dream book" to analyze them. I kept the book on the floor by my bed and when I work up before I could forget the dream, I'd look it up in the book to see what the dream meant. Muddy water or an unsettled sea meant that I had problems. Calm weather and clear water meant all is well. If I dreamed of a snake it meant I had an enemy. I go to where when I would dream of a snake if it was alive, I'd tell myself I had to kill it before I woke up. This way I got rid of the enemy. If it was a dead snake you dreamed of, it was all right. The enemy had been destroyed.

I believed in that dream book and I still remember dreams from it today. If you dreamed of a baby it meant a death would be in the family in the near future. If you dreamed of a death—then it was the opposite—it meant that a baby was going to be born in the family. I am a firm believer that if a new baby is born that someone dies in the family within a year. If it is a boy baby then it would be a male to die. If a girl then a female would die. Think it over!!! It really did work that way because I used to say "I wonder who it will be this time?" It didn't happen every time but almost every time. Evolution?????

# Movies

When as children, my twin and I went to the movies a lot. We would go on Saturday and stay all afternoon. There would be a serial such as "Batman" or "Superman" that would be continued from week to week and would always leave you in suspense as to what was going to happen. Then there would be a comedy such as "Abbott and Costello" or "Our Gang". There was always a cartoon such as "Popeye" or "Daffy Duck" that was put out by Looney Tunes. The main attraction was usually a Western. We would stay and see them all twice. It would kill the whole afternoon and keep us out of trouble.

There were two theaters in town to choose from, (The *Strand* or the *Colonial*.) Through the week we would go on Monday night to the Colonial and then on Tuesday we would go to the Strand. Thursday was always a special movie that just ran for that day only. We always had to see those. Of course, we got in for 12 cents. We went to the movies three or four times a week until they discovered we were 13 years old. You got in for 12 cents until you were 12. One day they stopped us and asked us our age and we were 13 so they let us in that time and from then on it would cost a quarter. That stopped our movie going so often.

The Colonial theater ran a contest one time to see how to improve attendance in the afternoon. Tommie and I entered. We both won five dollars for our suggestions. Mine was to make the price to get in cheaper in the afternoon than at night. They started that and it continues today at other theaters. *So* I guess I had a hand in the rates now used. Come to find out, only six people had entered the contest and they gave us all a prize. I don't know what Tommie suggested.

We went faithfully every Saturday to the movies. When we were about eleven our mother decided there was something better to do with our time rather than go to the movies. She told us we couldn't go anymore. We went to our dad and he said "NO" also—no more movies on Saturday. We both *started to show out in general*. We cried and begged and cried some more. Our dad couldn't stand the pressure, so he gave in. He gave us the money and told us to run as fast as we could and not look back before your mom sees you. We ran as fast as we could and stopped at the church to hide and catch our breath. To the movies we went. Of course our Mom told us that was a mean trick and not to repeat it. That really stopped our Saturday movie going.

When we went to the movies, we would stop at the dime store for candy. It was cheaper there. We would get a bag full. We would all get a different kind to see who got the most. Next time we would get that kind. It came out that marshmallow candy shaped like a peanut was the best buy. We also went to the variety store that was run by an old couple without children. They had a glass candy case and they looked for us every Saturday. Their candy was different from what the dime store sold. They always gave us good measure for our money. We didn't go there all the time because we felt they were giving us more candy on purpose and we didn't want to take advantage of them.

We used to get a candy called a "B-B Bat". It cost a penny and was pink in color. It was shaped long and narrow, approximately ½ inch across and about 5 inches long. You had to suck on it to get it soft before you could eat it because it was so hard. Another favorite was the "Sugar Daddy". This candy today is made also in "Sugar Babies". The sucker was also about 2 ½ inches across and about 5 ½ inches long. It was coated with chocolate. The center was a hard caramel that had to be sucked on to soften before you could eat it. It was referred to as an "all day sucker" as it would sometimes take that long to eat it. It would last through a movie. If we were low on cash, we would buy this sucker instead of candy that could be eaten faster. Both of these suckers are long instead of round as suckers are today. The "Sugar Daddy" cost all of 5 cents and the "BB Bat" cost a penny. We ate a lot of candy growing up as we were to busy to stop for "real food". I am sure this made the local dentists happy.

# Canton First Baptist Church

As children we joined the First Baptist Church in Canton and attended regularly. We went to Sunday School in the morning and stayed for morning worship. We also attended the G.A. 's. It was an organization for the girls. It seemed like every time they would plan an extra activity, something would interfere and we would not get to do it. I remember one time we were going on a hay ride. At the very last minute they called and canceled it as they couldn't get any hay or anything to ride in. I don't remember us getting to go to anything except the meetings that were held through the week in the afternoon.

As we got older we still went to church and to Baptist Training Union at night. It was always held before the church service. We always stayed for church and we always sat on the back row. There would be about 6 to 8 of us. We were about 11 or 12 years old. Our parents did not got to church at night as much as we children did. Now—this is the twins I am referring to. I don't remember my other brothers or sisters going as they were a little older than us. The other children involved in this episode were just neighbor children.

Well—there was a lady who sang in the choir at night and she always came out first and led the choir out. She always sang louder than the other choir members. Anyway, she was not only loud but her voice would tremble and she could be heard over the others and she would hold the notes longer than the others. I am sure by herself she had a beautiful voice but in a group she just stood out. It just struck us kids as being funny and we would get tickled every time. It would be worse when they sang their special song. We would "giggle" all the way through it.

The deacons, after taking up the collection, started bringing chairs and placing them behind the row we were on. We always sat on the back row. When we laughed they would tap us on the shoulder to quiet us down. We really tried to stop as we knew we shouldn't but you know how kids are!!! One starts and the others follow. We finally decided we had better stop or it might get out to our parents and we would be in trouble sure enough. At least we were in church and it did help shape our young lives. I can still hear that lady singing today, and I smile.

We joined the church during a revival along with other children our age. We were about twelve years old. We were baptized on Sunday following the revival. We wore white dresses and I still remember the dress clinging to our body when we came up out of the water. The water was very warm. We made a wet mess on the floor in a back room of the church with all that water dripping off of us. Tommie and I also sang in the children's choir. We sang at the night service so many nights a month. The older folks sang in the choir that sang at the morning worship hour.

# Church Outing—Swimming Pool

The church was about a five minute walk from our house. You could see it from our yard. Our Sunday School teacher took us on an outing to a swimming pool. One of the first outside swimming

*Buzz at the famous swimming pool where I saw the snake. Above his head on the side of the pool is where the snake was, it is marked with an "X."*

pools in Canton belonged to a family that lived several miles from our house. It was out in the country and we could either walk the road or take a shortcut through a pasture.

I had rather have gone the long way by the road but I followed the crowd through the pasture. Well—there was this big mean looking bull in the pasture and it was eyeing us. This, in turn made my heart pound and I sure wished they changed their minds and went by the road. We had to climb the fence in order to get in the pasture. There was no gate close by. Of course, one of us got caught on the barbed wire that ran across the top of the fence. The bull being there encouraged us to move fast to get out of there to safety. Did we ever walk fast and keep an eye on the bull until we got out of there!!! Or at least I did!!!.

The swimming pool was made from concrete and the water to keep it filled ran by gravity by a pipe from the top of the mountain. The water was icy cold but it didn't matter as we were usually hot from walking in the sun. After we got in and got wet we didn't care so much about the cold. We would swim awhile and then we would eat our lunch we had taken with us.

We were charged admission to the pool which was about a nickel or a dime. They had a small concession stand that sold drinks. The drinks were usually about half warm as they just cooled them in ice. No ice cream as they couldn't keep it from thawing. We would spend the day there.

One day I was swimming around and decided to get out of the pool. You couldn't stay in long because of the cold water. When you got out your teeth would chatter. There was a rail that ran around the inside of the pool that was probably there for the over flow from the pool. We would hold on to it to help hold us up in the water when we got tired and wanted to rest.

One day I reached for the rail but something seemed to be in the way where I wanted to lay my hand to catch on. I pulled my hand back and just looked a minute to see if it was a stick of wood or something else lying there. After looking closer I realized it was a snake. It didn't move—but I did!! Talk about getting out of there, by swimming across to where the ladder was. Of course, the teacher made light of it. I wasn't to keen to swim there after that. Just think, if it was on the rail in the pool, it was bound to swim in there too.

Later the town built an outside pool for the public. I learned to swim at the YMCA pool and I preferred to swim there after the snake incident. So—my whole summer wasn't ruined. My brother, "Buzz" used to swim at the outside pool a lot, especially after mowing yards all day and he was "hot."

# Hair Cut

As a teen you want to look your best especially if you are in love, or think you are. I did mention earlier that I was struck on one of the doctor's sons. I decided I needed a hair cut and I didn't have the money to go to the beauty shop so my twin sister volunteered to do it. I wanted it cut short behind. Well, she cut it short behind all right, so short I couldn't roll it on curlers or anything.

Sometimes we would roll our hair on strips of paper torn from a brown paper grocery bag. My hair was so short it would not even roll on that. It was cut almost as short as a man's hair behind. Paper strips would make your hair look so pretty and you could sleep with them in your hair because they were soft. If you kept it rolled all night it would keep the curl longer.

I was so ashamed of that haircut I wore a scarf for what seemed like all summer to hide it and I avoided my heart throb. He probably couldn't care less as to how I looked. I wouldn't play outside with the kids until it grew some. It was pure agony to be in the house and hearing them playing and me in the house. I swore she cut it on purpose.

I saved my money I earned by babysitting until I had the price of a perm which was twelve dollars. The beautician, I believe, knew my problem because she said it wasn't hardly long enough to roll but she would try. After all I was wearing that stupid scarf when I came into the shop. My hair turned out real pretty and I could have hugged that beautician for giving me back a life. My summer wasn't totally ruined.

Keeping your hair curled was a problem. No set or hair spray was available. If our hair was curly when we left home for school, and it was foggy, you better believe it would be "limp" when we got to school. If we wore a scarf it helped some. We learned to keep our hair pin-curled on the side and take it down after we got to school. I found that strips of brown paper bag curled your hair the best and you could sleep when you turned over. I found it best to let your hair get almost dry and just slightly damp before you rolled it and it would dry quicker. "Toni" perms were the go. You gave them to yourself at home. Usually they were more "fuzzy" than curl.

# Sexual Harrassment

We now come to the subject of sexual harassment. If the stories that follow fit, then there was sexual harassment in the 1930's-1950's. It will show that it's not something new.

As children, we went to the movies a lot. We had the habit, if the movie theater wasn't full, we would change seats a lot to see the picture from different places in the theater. One day I was doing just that. I sat down in a dark area of the theater to watch the show when a man came and sat down by me. He could have sat further away as there were other seats but he sat down right by me. Well—he doesn't seem to be watching the movie. It seemed he kept touching my leg. I thought it was accidental but he kept doing it. He proceeded to unzip his pants and started to put his hand in his pants. Well—talk about getting up and climbing over the seat back and getting the heck out of there pronto!! I never saw him again.

Another time we were playing at a friends house in a big barn behind their house. We were playing in the bottom in the hay. We were throwing hay at each other and laughing and having a big time. All of a sudden we felt a drop of water dripping from above from the hay loft. We didn't pay much attention until it got a little heavier. We looked up to see what it was and couldn't see anything. We climbed the ladder and there was her brother and he was laughing. He had "wet" above us and thought it was funny. Luckily, he didn't get any on us.

I attended the First Baptist Church as a child. On Sunday night we had Baptist Training Union for the youth. It always met before the church service. We used to play around the church and run and play after it was over, between then and the church service. One night we were doing this and as we passed the furnace room in the basement we noticed a light burning. Standing under it was the janitor. His hands were at the front of his pants and he was doing "something" with them. We really couldn't see anything but he was making a vulgar motion. He was noticed doing this on more than one occasion. The boys used to lay out of church and sneak around and see if he was there, and sure enough—he was.

He seemed to know when someone was watching. If I was walking to town, if he was in the church yard and saw me, he would go in that room and there he would be when I passed the church. I would avoid looking that way. I finally quit going that way to town. I took a longer way on another street.

# Our Picture

My Mom decided to get our picture taken at a studio in Asheville. She had to call and set up an appointment beforehand. She was going to have her picture made too.

The day before the appointment, Tommie and I were sent to the beauty shop to get our hair set for the occasion. Our Mom went in the afternoon after we had ours set that morning. She told us she was going to get her hair cut and have a permanent. We had never seen

*Mama's fingerwave and our limp hair. Note one of our bows is up-side-down.*

her wear her hair any way but pulled straight back in a bun at the back of her head or else it would be braided and put on top of her head.

Everyone was excited and couldn't wait for her to come home. We watched the road for her and finally the wait was over. Here she came and out we went to meet her, as we couldn't wait for her to get to the house. As I got closer to her I noticed her hair looked the same only it had a "finger wave" and was still pulled back with the bun still at the back of her head.

I said, "I thought you were getting your hair cut!"

She said, "I did."

I couldn't believe that so I said, "Where?"

She said, "In the back. I had two inches cut off."

Well, with her hair so long it touched her hips, two inches sure wasn't missed.

The next morning we got up to catch the bus to Asheville. It had rained the night before and it was damp and foggy. When we got to Asheville it was really foggy. When we got to the studio the fog and dampness had done it's thing because our hair looked a sight. All the curl was nearly gone and it was limp and damp. The lady at the studio tried to "fix" our hair. She did the best she could. We had our picture made anyway, limp hair and all.

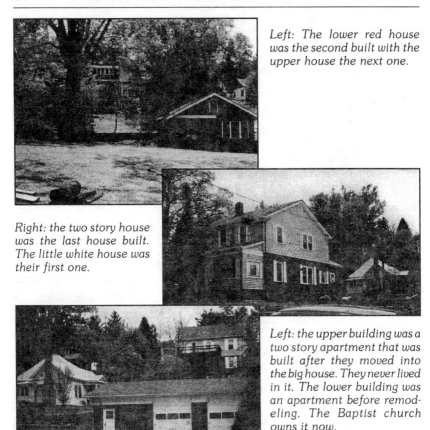

Left: The lower red house was the second built with the upper house the next one.

Right: the two story house was the last house built. The little white house was their first one.

Left: the upper building was a two story apartment that was built after they moved into the big house. They never lived in it. The lower building was an apartment before remodeling. The Baptist church owns it now.

# Houses

There was a couple who lived in our community that, I guess, you could describe as unusual. He worked in the mill but he also had houses built to rent. He built a total of six. They were built from the time I can remember until I was about ten years old. Every time he had a house built his wife would have them moved into it and they would live there until he built another one. Then they would move into that house. He finally remodeled a two-story house next door to the Baptist church and they lived in it until they both died. She must have liked that one. I had several playmates who lived in these houses. I did baby-sitting with some of them.

# Bike

My brother "Buzz" first worked at the local hardware store. We had two in town. He bought us our first pair of skates for Christmas from there. They were one gift that was well used. We wore them out on the concrete streets of our neighborhood. The neighborhood kids would gather and we would skate all afternoon just about every day it was pretty. We learned to skate backwards, jump cracks, jump cracks backwards even going down hills. I don't remember anyone getting hurt. Just think we were Olympic material for we sure got enough practice.

"Buzz" also bought a second-hand bicycle that he would lock with a bicycle chain and lock. Well, not to be outdone, we learned how to get it off and would attempt to ride it while he was at work. My sister would hold the seat of the bicycle and walk beside me and then I would do her the same way. One day I thought she had the seat and she had turned it loose without me knowing it. That is how I learned to ride. Off I would go unattended. What a great feeling to be riding by yourself!

After I married and our boys got old enough to learn to ride a bicycle my husband bought them a new bike. One day he came home from work and had a brand new bike in the truck bed. They didn't take to it right away. They didn't show any interest in it so one day when he came home from working the day shift he told them if they didn't learn to ride that bike he was going to give it away. Those two boys got that bike out and learned to ride it in no time flat. It was late in the day when they started to learn. At ten o'clock at night they were still riding that bike in the dark. They had to take turns as there was only one. He later got them another bike so they both could ride at the same time. You could hear them out in the dark yelling to each other as they rode. It was a gravel road and no light except the moon, if it happened to be out.

# The Woods

When I was growing up everyone knew everyone else in town. We were just like a big happy family. My mom visited with her friends a lot and she always took Tommie and me with her.

One day when walking home from one of these visits we walked by the cemetery and through a small wooded area. We passed a Birch tree and my Mom broke off a piece and proceeded to break it in short pieces. She gave one each to Tommie and me and kept one for herself. She told us to chew it and it would get soft so we could use it for a tooth brush. She explained the chewing is what cleaned our teeth. The taste wasn't too bad.

I saw this pretty leaf and started to pick it when she grabbed my hand to stop me. That's how I learned about poison oak. She showed me the difference between it and other plants. It was late in the day being almost dark and I remember the experience well. We also were shown sassafras and other plants and trees.

We played with a girl that lived near the cemetery. One day we discovered that blackberries were ripe. There was a bush that was across the road from her house on a small hill. We could sit there and

*The piano with Dee in the chair.*

look down on her house. We ate them from the bush until we got tired of them so we decided to make a blackberry drink. She went home and brought back a glass jar. We put our berries in it and then mashed them with a stick. To this we added a little water. When we tasted it, —boy— was it sour! She talked me into sneaking home and getting the sugar because she knew her Mom wouldn't let her have any. It was rationed at the time, because of the war. You only got, like a 5 lb. bag a month. So we fixed our drink and you know—it really wasn't so great! I remember it was hot. Some ice might have helped it.

We also played hide and seek in the cemetery. Not very often however, as it was too spooky. After dark you can imagine things that aren't there. And tales told us about drunks stopping there to sleep by a tomb rock. We were also told about graves sinking and we might fall in one of them. And, of course, the best one of all was the ghosts being there after dark.

# Piano

We had a giant black piano that stood in the corner of our living room. It literally took up ¼ of the room. My Mom used to play it and sing religious songs sometimes. She was a very religious lady. Her dad was a self-made preacher. I tried to play the piano and sometimes played "Chop Sticks" and little tunes I would make up. I never took lessons, I guess because with so many children, that money was scarce.

My older sisters offered to pay for Tommie and I to take lessons after they went to college and got a job, but by then we would be behind everyone else we knew that took lessons.

We were also to the age that other things were more important than that. Or so it seemed to us. You know how teenagers are!

# Teenage Crush

When I was 15, I started to work in one of the local 10 cent stores. One summer I worked, there was a young manager

*My teenage crush. He signed the picture: To Jo, my pal.*

trainee that came from Tennessee to work at the store. I thought he was the best looking man I had ever seen. We got along fine. I couldn't wait to get to work. Of course, he didn't know I had a crush on him. I kept it to myself. Then this good-looking black-haired beauty came to work across the street at the local printing office. He started dating her. After that I lost interest. He worked there all summer and then went back to Tennessee. He gave me his picture to keep. Just another disappointment in life!!! Life's full of them.

# Teen Diary

I kept a diary of my senior year in high school. Sometimes I get it out and read it and it's like going back in time and reliving it. I wrote of ballgames and of crushes on boys, some of which were ballplayers. Some from other schools and I can't even remember their names.

My bosom buddy, Peggy, was about the only one with a car. Cars were scarce then and the only reason she had one to drive was that her dad worked as a timber buyer and he was provided with a car by Champion, allowing the family car to be available. So being an only child, she sorta got what she wanted.

We went to all the ballgames—be it softball, football, or basketball. We went to all of the tournaments at home and out of town as well.

Her dad took us to the out of town night games whether there was snow, rain, or blizzard, as long as they played. I earned my money for admission at the ten cent store where I worked on Saturdays. We went to the game on Tuesday night and then again on Thursday. Football was always on Friday night. We didn't miss a game.

When all my school buddies and my sister went off to college I was left home alone. I knew my dad would have trouble sending two of us to college at the same time so I just said I didn't want to go—so my twin could go. All the boys who didn't go to college worried me to death to date them. I had my choice. However, I was in love with only one, so I dated some for the heck of it to keep from staying home all the time. They were all nice dates.

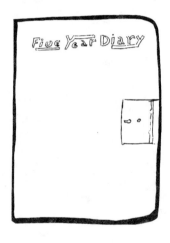

Smoking was not allowed during school hours nor were we supposed to leave the school grounds during school hours. There was one particular group of girls and boys who left every day at lunch. They were called into the Principal's office and expelled for two weeks. Talk about the whole school being shook up. That was the big news for the day.

Peggy could drive her dad's car to school and back home after school but no other time during school hours. It was usually packed with all who could get in it. She like to smoke and she couldn't smoke and drive so she let me drive. We always went the back roads to Bethel. I need to mention this was after everyone had gone home from school and we were alone.

This helped me in later years to get my driver's license. I passed with no problems and have yet to have an accident. Well—a serious one!!! The very next week after I got my license I was driving around and happened to see a field full of little pink pigs with their mother. The next thing I know I'm in a ditch. I got out without any problem. I just drove right back onto the road. It taught me to pay attention when behind the wheel. You can't sightsee and drive too until you are more experienced.

# My First Job

As a child of twelve, I began my first job. It was babysitting with a six months old baby. I went to their house at one o'clock and stayed until six in the evening.

While the baby slept, I was to wash the dishes, and there were plenty. It looked like a full day of dirty dishes saved just for me to wash. I washed them by hand and dried them and put them up. There was no dishwasher. At first I just washed them and left them to dry in the drain but I was informed the next day that they were to be put on the shelves instead.

The lady I was baby sitting for would wash in the morning and leave the clothes on the line for me to bring in and fold. There were usually two lines of them at least. When the baby woke up, I had to dry him and then feed him his cereal or baby food and then give him a bottle. He would stay awake then until his mother came home. I did all of this for two dollars a week.

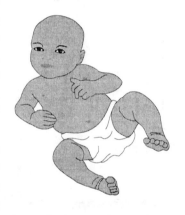

My twin, Tommie, kept two boys who lived across the street from where I baby sat. In fact, I believe I got my job because of Tommie. She didn't have to do all the work I had to. She got to sit in the yard and watch the two boys play and even got refreshments. I was never left refreshments. I don't remember even having time to stop to eat anything. I stayed so busy. I always seemed to get the worst end of the deal, or so it seemed to me.

I also washed dishes for our next door neighbor for fifty cents. It's funny how you will work away from home and actually enjoy it. I hated washing dishes at home. I guess because there were so many more at our house because my mom could dirty more pots and they were always greasy. After all, she had a big family to cook for. Kitchens were always hot especially in the summer.

Don't give up on kids because they won't work at home, because it doesn't necessarily mean they are lazy.

*Rose's Dime Store, the brown building on the left.*

# Teen Job

When I was fifteen years old our local Rose's dime store burned down. We woke up to the excitement of a fire having taken place while we slept. It was a big event in our little town. When it was being rebuilt we kids would look at it and walk through it after the workers had gone home. No one said anything to us. Things weren't stolen back then as readily as it is today.

When I found out that they were taking applications to work, I applied for a job. Being underage I was sent to the court house to get a worker's permit that had to be signed by my parents. Several of the kids from school applied for work. They hired a bunch of us. I went to work before it opened to the public by marking merchandise and even helped put the counters together and displaying the merchandise.

On opening day there were about as many clerks as there were customers. It was a big day. My twin sister and some of our friends worked there. I continued to work part-time after school and on Saturdays until I graduated from high school. I even worked during the summer for two summers.

Some of the other girls got laid off after the opening day rush. They kept me, however. Tommie was one that they let go. I always tried to look busy when the customers were down but the other girls including Tommie would just stand around and talk. I worked on every counter in the store and even worked in the stock room making Easter baskets. I even got to work the candy counter and weigh candy. I made 25 cents an hour.

One year a lady came in and had merchandise put away on lay-away for Christmas. It was a little early to do this but anyway we did it for her. It was put on a high shelf in the lay-away department in the stock room and her name placed on it. When she came in on Christmas Eve to get it, it was nowhere to be found. It had been put out and sold. The manager had to help her get other gifts. This taught me a lesson. Just because it's on lay-away does not mean it will be there when you go for it.

Since there were no air conditioners back then, there were fans placed over the doors right inside the entrance. One day a lady came in and just as she walked inside a paddle off of the fan came off and hit her in the forehead. The fans weren't covered with anything for protection in case the paddle came loose. Her injury wasn't severe but she sued the store anyway.

Guess who just about got to go to court? You are right!!! Me!! I just happened to be working at the front counter the day it happened and saw it happen. I had to come to work prepared to go to court after lunch if I was needed. By luck, it was settled out of court. Talk about sweating it out that morning at work waiting to hear from them.

One Saturday, I wanted off for two hours to go to the beauty shop to get my hair "set". The manager wouldn't let me off but she let off a girl that just worked part-time. She said she couldn't spare me as that was a busy time of the day. So—when I went to lunch—I just didn't go back to work. I'd show her!!! I was tired of everyone else loafing and me having to work all the time. I was tired of the dime store anyway. I had graduated from High School and wanted bigger and better things.

From there I went to work at the American Enka plant that made nylon for hosiery and gowns. They also made carpet yarn. We went to the personnel office and applied one Monday morning, got a physical and went home.

We were hired to start the graveyard shift that night. There were several of us, about five in all. We had went to apply together and we all got a job. Being young I didn't sleep well in the daytime. I was afraid that I would miss something. My friend, Peggy, would call me at about 11 o'clock to go to ride around town with her and up I would get and go with her. She went to college in the fall but when she was home we still loafed together.

After several months not getting enough sleep caught up with me. My brother's wife worked there too and one Saturday we decided to stay up and go to Asheville shopping. After we got home instead of going to bed like I should have I stayed up and went to the local hangout which was the ice cream parlor. A schoolmate had gotten killed in a car wreck the night before and we were talking about it when I started getting dizzy and my vision was blurry.

Guess who just fainted dead away? Me—of course!! Someone at another table had noticed me falling out of the chair and grabbed me before I hit the floor. Well, the best looking boy took me home. He carried me up the steps to the house in his arms. My dad was home alone at the time. They put me to bed. Of course, Tommie and two of our girl friends were tagging along behind. I wanted to get up and go back to town but they wouldn't let me.

My dad wouldn't let me go back to work at Enka anymore. He said if I wasn't going to take care of myself then he'd just have to. I didn't argue with him as the night shift wasn't for me. There was no rotating shifts. I was supposed to work graveyard all the time. I would be so sleepy when on the bus to work. I resented it that everyone else was going to bed but me. I had to stay up all night.

My third job was at Belk Hudson's Department Store. I sold everything from clothes, ribbon, hose, pocketbooks, shoes, cloth, thread, and even men's clothes. I worked there about two years.

A high school friend of mine worked for one of the local doctors. When she got married and was going to quit work, she recommended me to the doctor to take her place. She came to the store and asked me if I was interested. It sounded like a good change so I talked to the Manager and he let me quit without working a notice. He was very nice about it.

I started my new job on Monday morning. She had asked me on Thursday, so I finished out the week with Belk's. She gave me her white uniforms and showed me what I was supposed to do. My day started by dusting the office and straightening the magazines. When I am in a waiting room now I notice the magazines and if they are straight. Then I had to sterilize the metal needles and glass syringes. There were no disposable ones then. We used the same ones over and over and sterilized them between each use. I did the lab work that consisted of checking urine and blood. We used a little slanted knife to prick the finger to check the blood. I was always afraid that I would "jab" it too deep and hit the bone. I never did though.

I remember Tommie having a "bone felon" from an injury to her finger and how it was swollen and painful. She cried with it and finally had to go to the doctor and have it treated. I don't know who dreaded the stick worse, me or the patient. I checked the hemoglobin of the blood by a chart according to where the color fit. I also used the microscope but I wasn't very good at that. The doctor would view it after I set it up for him.

I was also the bookkeeper and I mailed out the statements each month. He would tell me who to send them to. If he felt they were paying all they could he would let it ride for another month. I learned a lot about human nature working there. The people with the most were the worst to let their bills go unpaid. The poorer folks usually paid cash or paid an amount every month though it was small. He never sent them a bill as long as they were paying anything at all.

When someone came in to get a vaccine for their baby, I would have to go to the health department to get it. It was free to the doctors but you had to pay the doctor who gave it. That's how I learned to go straight to the health department first and save money when my children needed "shots." They always kept a good record when they were given. They probably still have my children on their records now.

I would keep the light out in the office unless the doctor was there. He told me one day that his light bill had gone down after I came to work for him. He asked me "what are you doing different?" I told him and he said it was all right as long as the reception room lights were on. He had a fish aquarium but he kept it cleaned. It was an all day job. I was glad I didn't have to help with it. He came in on his day off and cleaned it.

I was dating Bill then and when he went to work, he would always come by the office, slow down, and blow his car horn at me. He did this before he went in to work at 3 p.m. and if he was working days he would come by after 3 p.m. This always made my day go better. I worked for this doctor for about two years until I married. I worked for $18.00 per week.

When the mill was putting out it's famous fallout, the front of my uniform that I was so proud of would get speckled with it. Little black specks or dots would be all over the front of my clean uniform. This happened usually in the morning only. I finally got a clear plastic raincoat that I would wear over my uniform when I suspected a fallout. I wanted to keep my precious uniform clean. The raincoat cost all of $2.00. My uniforms were sent to the laundry and I could wear them twice as the starch kept them clean longer than if I had just washed them at home. It only cost 25 cents to get them laundered and ready to wear.

I watched the doctor lance a pimple on this boy's face one time. When he came in his face was all swollen and I thought he had an abscessed tooth. It turned out when it was lanced that about ½ cup of pus came out of it and the biggest core I had ever seen. I really enjoyed helping when he had to put stitches in. He was kind of shaky and he was slow. I wanted to get ahold of that needle and do the sewing. In fact, one day I asked him if I could. He replied "Well, I don't care but if it was found out I would lose my license."

I also gave arthritis IV injections even when the doctor wasn't there. It would be a series of ten and after the first one was given by the doctor I gave the rest. If they came in and he wasn't there, I just went ahead and gave them. Don't ask me what it was because I don't remember. It must not have worked as I haven't heard of it being used today.

Speaking on injections, we both got a "Bug" one winter as one was going around. He asked me to give him an antibiotic injection and then he would give me one. I didn't like that idea too well so I gave him his but I declined the offer of me getting one. After he went to lunch you will never guess what I did!! I gave myself a shot in my hip while he was gone. I wasn't stealing as he offered to give it to me. I just didn't want him doing it. That could get a little uncomfortable. It had to be given deep in the muscle and that meant pulling down my under panties. All he had to do was pull his pants at the back down a little. Mine was a whole different ball game.

# Walking

We walked everywhere. We would walk to the Post Office at least twice a day, just to have something to do. We knew exactly when the mail would "run" and we would go and check to see if we got anything. It "ran" in the morning and then again at 4 o'clock in the afternoon.

We weren't allowed to walk near the bus stop. It was during World War II and servicemen caught the bus there and also got off the bus when they came in on furlough. My parents said it didn't look nice to be around there. So we would cross the street when we got near it to avoid it.

The only thing was—that was the only place we could get popcorn when we went to the movies—was at the bus stop. (We called it the Soda Shop.) The movie theater was next door to the Soda Shop. We would get one of us to watch and the other one would go as fast as they could to get the corn and back before we were seen. Later the theater installed their own popcorn machine.

We walked to the swimming pool in town just to have something to do and to see who was there. It was nothing to see kids walking on the streets all the time. That was their only means of transportation. Now you would be talked about if you walked. We walked to school and to all of the ballgames at night.

*Jody, (myself) at the post office getting the mail. The year was 1947—I was a Junior in High School.*

# High School

When I was in high school we always walked to school. If it was raining we walked, if it was foggy or snowy we walked. When it was foggy our hair always lost it's curl unless we kept it rolled until we got there. No hair spray to help out. Snow didn't keep us from going to school. We rarely got out for snow days. After school we came by one of the drug stores for a snack. They

Jody —Me.

all had soda fountains then. We would all crowd in one of them and all three were always full for about one hour then all would be quiet again.

As we walked up the hill to our separate houses we had to pass the funeral home. One day in particular the guy working there asked us if we wanted a "tour". Of course, we did. He took us through the building where they embalmed the bodies on the cold slab and the viewing rooms.

Next he took us to the big building in the back. There were four of us girls. This was where they stored the coffins. The lighting was poor and nearly dark. He hadn't turned any lights on. We were looking around and walking among them. All of a sudden someone said, "What are you doing?" We all jumped of course thinking it was a dead man speaking. It lucked out that wasn't the case. It was "Jim" Wells, the owner. He had seen us go in and came out to visit with us. He always kept chewing gum in his pocket to give away. If you passed the funeral home and he was on the porch he would say "Little Pac" come here. Up we would go to him and out came the gum. He was known to us as the gum man.

In high school our classes were divided up into semesters. One ended at Christmas and the other one was when school was out. We took General Science one semester and the next one we took Home Economics. Home Economics was divided into sewing for one half of the course and cooking the last half. I made a blouse. We just cut

*In 1948 this building was the Canton High School.*

it out and sewed it. I don't remember the teacher checking on our work unless we took it to her. She usually just sat in a chair in the middle of the room and if we needed her help she was there. The cooking part was just as bad. We were taught to make "prune whip". We would cook the prunes, mash them, then fold beaten egg whites into them. It was all right I guess. But it didn't make enough of an impression on me to make me want to make it again.

# College

After I graduated from high school I continued to work at Hudson's while Tommie went off to college at Pfeiffer. My dad tried to get me to go to Cecil's Business College in Asheville but I wouldn't go. I knew it was expensive and hard to have two in college at the same time. It had been two of everything while we were in school. Two class rings, two annuals—after all we were twins.

So—I stayed home and worked and fell in love and got married. Within the first year I had my first child. When I wrote my twin sister that I had a baby—they told me that when she got the letter and read it, she stayed in bed and out of class. I guess they were trying to tell me that she was upset. I found this all out later, in the meantime I was perfectly happy in my new life.

I remember writing to her before my son was born to tell her all about the country. I wrote "It seems like everything here is reproducing. Me, our dog had pups, our cat had kittens, our chickens were hatching out little chickens and our cow had a new calf." It was all new to me and I was full of the wonder at it all.

# Square Dancing

As a teen I liked to square dance. The only catch was that they were held in another town from ours. As cars were scarce we had to catch the bus or catch a ride with friends. We would all "pile" in the car, if we found someone that would take us, with just as many as it would hold and more.

One such Saturday, my twin and two of our friends from the country, who were spending the night with us, decided we wanted to go to the square dance. We had worked that day at the local dime store. Our friends usually stayed with us and went home on Sunday. The bus they would have to catch ran after work at 11 o'clock at night, so they just stayed the night and caught the 3 o'clock bus home the next day.

Town was quiet this night and prospects looked grim for getting a ride. We were walking around feeling sad because it looked like we weren't going to get to go to Waynesville. We made up—to separate and go opposite directions and see if we could bum a ride. We walked about everywhere we went so no one thought a thing about it. Well— Sarah and myself were walking along the sidewalk in front of one of the stores—when a pale blue convertible slowed down by us with two males in it. They yelled "Hello." Sarah yelled "hello" back to him. They asked "want a lift?" Sarah replied with "sure, we want to go to the square dance, are you going that way?" They said "Sure, get in." Which we did.

Everything happened so fast I couldn't object. She told them we had two more girls to get—that were with us. They didn't seem too happy about that—but we stopped and picked them up anyway. All four of us girls got in the back seat, leaving the boys up front alone.

We were riding along and my sister whispered "who are these boys?" I said "I don't know but I think Sarah knows them." Sarah looked at me surprised and said, "I don't know them. I thought you did."

Well—with this revelation we were about ready to make them stop the car and let us out. It was our only hope of getting to the dance and if we stayed together we would probably be all right. Well—the boys started in a different direction than the way to the square dance. Out came a bottle of whiskey. We began to get scared and told them they were going the wrong way. The acted like they didn't hear us. Then one of them suggested that one of us get in the front seat to make it more comfortable in the back. Sarah decided since she was the biggest, that she would. She convinced them that we wanted to go to the square dance—to please let us out. They decided to take us where we wanted to go. They took us to the square dance and let us out. They didn't go in. We found out later that they were both married. We caught the bus home after the dance. You better believe we didn't do that again. We only accepted a ride from people we knew from school.

# Spanish Class

My mom had to have surgery to have her gallbladder removed when I was in the tenth grade in high school. She never fully recovered from that surgery. She never was the same as far as being active. She seemed to feel bad a lot. She would get up in the morning and get my dad off to work and then she would go back to bed. We would get up and get ourselves off to school. After all, we were the ninth and tenth child to go to school. I guess she was tired out at that point.

She would leave our breakfast on the stove or the table. If it was on the stove it was cold oatmeal as the fire would be low and the oatmeal would get cold. I usually didn't eat it. If our breakfast was on the table it was a jar of canned cold blackberries to eat with cream and sugar with biscuits crumbled up in it. It was usually pretty good. These breakfasts didn't help my learning process, however. I was usually starved in the class right before lunch and my stomach would "growl" sometimes right loudly. I would hold my hand over my stomach to try to keep the sound down.

*George from Chile, South America.*

It didn't help my concentration on Spanish very well. I didn't make the grades I would have liked to but I guess it couldn't be helped. I used to eat two or three pieces of loaf bread just to have something in my stomach hoping to ward off the hunger. We didn't have toasters then so I couldn't make toast.

In our Spanish class we had pen pals from South America that we wrote to. We wrote to them in Spanish and they wrote back in Spanish.

After I married, one day I went home to visit my mom. There was a letter there for me from a boy I had written to from Chile. He was writing to tell me he was coming to the states to go to school in Chapel Hill, North Carolina. He wanted me to write and give him my telephone number so he could call me and come to see me. I never answered the letter or I never told my husband about it either. He might not understand. I just forgot about it. I wonder what would have happened if I wasn't married. I could have been living in Chile in South America instead of in the country. But then I wouldn't have all these great adventures to write about.

# Wild Night

We went to the square dance at the armory in Waynesville although our parents did not approve of it. One Saturday night, I had a date and we went to the dance. While there a couple invited us to their house to a party after the square dance. It was on our way home. We couldn't decided whether to go or not. A friend that was there wanted to go so we took her with us and went to the couple's house.

This happened in the 40's right after World War II. Cars were still few as the auto industry had not gotten back into production yet. They had been converted to make planes and tanks for the war. It was common for people to "bum" a ride somewhere.

When we got to the party, the driveway was full of cars. We went in and no one even noticed us. Man—what a party!!! Everyone was having a big time. They had left the square dance before it was over. It wasn't over until midnight. We liked to dance so we stayed until it was over. Back to the party—in the kitchen—it was a mess.

The men had gotten hungry and tried to build a fire in the kitchen stove. Well—as they had had a few drinks they were staggering around and one of the men had fallen against the stove pipe as they were building the fire and had knocked the stove pipe loose and there was smoke everywhere. The guy trying to cook the eggs was having a hard time as the pan was cold and they were just a slimy mess.

Some of the women had already gone to bed. There were two to three to a bed. They appeared to be passed out. Someone had poured liquor into the fish bowl and the poor fish were drunk and could barely swim. The poor cat was also drunk as they had poured whiskey in it's bowl and it had drunk it. It was probably "white lighting" as it was still available then. You just had to know where to get it.

We stayed a while longer and then left. Too much for us!!! I don't think they even knew we were there. By the time we left the party it was getting late and we were hungry. We stopped at an all night "bar". When we drove into the parking lot, there were two men outside and they were "fist fighting" and you could plainly see that they had been drinking.

I thought, "Oh Boy"—I'm not going in there !! First of all, my mom would kill me if she knew I had went in there. I was also afraid of getting shot as it looked like a wild place. Bill and our friend went in but I stayed in the car.

After about thirty minutes Bill came back out and told me to come on in. It was quiet now. He had ordered me a hamburger and I was hungry. Sure enough—it was quiet with a juke box playing and people were dancing. It was very dim as the lights were very low. Needless to say, the hamburger was good and we didn't get shot as I had believed. We sat and listened to the music a while. The night was wearing on.

When we got to my house it was getting daylight. I didn't know what to do as my dad was due to get up anytime to go to work. I was afraid he would hear me going up those stupid creaky stairs and catch me for sure, and I would be in big trouble. I didn't dare tell Bill what I was thinking so I let him take me to the door as usual and I just stood on the steps until he left. I couldn't go into the house yet—I would have to hide somewhere until my dad left for work. My mom always went back to bed after my dad left. The only place I could think of to hide in quickly was the chicken house. We didn't have chickens then so the chicken house was fairly clean but a little dusty. The basement door was closed and I was afraid I would make a noise opening it. So I couldn't hide there.

Sure enough—I had just got settled down when on came the light in the house. I waited until my dad left and the light went back off. I knew it was safe after about thirty minutes—so I slipped into the house through the front door, as it was never locked. Guess what???? Lady luck was with me as the stairs did not squeak and I made it in the house without getting caught. My mom was sleeping soundly. So much for that night. It wasn't repeated as one night like that was enough for me.

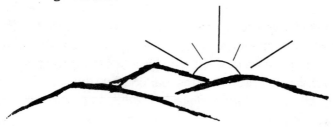

# Moonshine

Bill called me from work one day before we were married and asked me to go for a ride with him after he got off from work at 3 p. m. According to what he said he had an errand to run. He came after me and we started towards Waynesville. I didn't ask him where we were going as I felt he would have told me if he had wanted me to know.

We rode for awhile and then we took what I would refer to as "a back road". The road led us into a heavily wooded area and onto a single lane dirt road. It was more like a trail than a road. He stopped the car and got out. He told me to "just stay in the car. I'll be right back."

He was gone a short period of time when here he came carrying a brown bag with something in it. He was carrying it close to his body. He didn't say anything for awhile and then he said "it's best that you forget where you just went." If we are stopped you don't know what is in this bag."

Come to find out it was a ½ gallon jar of "White Lightening" or "Moonshine". He was getting it for some man he worked with. If caught, he could have been arrested and so could I. Luckily, we got home safe. That was the only time that happened but I think back on what the outcome would have been if we had been caught. He wanted me along so he wouldn't look suspicious going there alone.

# Courting

I was working for a doctor as his assistant when Bill and I were dating. The doctors office was upstairs over a clothing store. The windows looked out over the street. When the doctor was gone on his lunch hour, I would sit in the window and do my paper work.

When Bill worked 3 - 11 he would always drive by the office in his car. He would drive real slow until he got even with the window, then he would blow his horn and step on the gas and then go on to work. If he was going home after working 7 - 3, he did the same thing only it would be after 3. I looked forward to this and missed it when he was off work that day. He was a little shy, as he wasn't much with words.

# Forever Amber

I believe the first sexy movie I saw as a child was "Forever Amber" with Linda Darnell. That movie today is mild compared to what is shown on the movies today. Also Jane Russell was in a "dirty" movie. She wore a low ruffled peasant necked blouse and rolled in the hay with her male co-actor. Everybody was squirming in their seats. They thought they were really bad movies. I rather enjoyed them myself.

# II.

# MINI-MEMORIES

# Old Locust Field Academy

One of the first schools in Canton was called the "Old Academy". It was located where the present First Baptist church stands today. It was built after the Locust Field Church was founded. It was a gray two story square building. The older members of our family started school there.

When another better school was built of brick the old academy was abandoned. I stood in our front yard and watched as it was torn down. You might say that they just pulled it apart. That's what it looked like. All the walls fell at once. They had tied the walls to a big machine and pulled on it until it fell. I can still see the gray dust that filled the sky as it fell. The sound of it falling to my child's ears was very loud. I wondered what we would do without the old building standing there.

# Spring Cleaning

Every spring our beds were taken apart and taken to the back of the house to be cleaned. They were iron beds with metal frames. They had metal springs that the cotton mattress would lay on. The springs would get dusty and could harbor spiders and other "varmints." They would be scalded with hot water to kill the bugs and germs.

If the "ticking" was getting too old, it would be replaced. It was always navy blue striped with white and very heavy. Our pillows were also covered with this same material. Our pillows would usually be made from chicken feathers picked from our chickens. I still have one of those pillows.

In fact, I made one small one for each of my grandchildren. Those feathers are about 55 years old. They still make a good pillow. The cloth would be sewed up like a pillow case with one end left open to put the mattress or pillow back into. It would then be sewed up on the end.

The bed springs would be leaned up against the house to dry and sun after they were washed. The "ticking" or cover would be washed and hung on the line to sun all day. I would make myself scarce on this day if I could. I hated this chore.

# First Grade

I remember learning my ABC's in the first grade. I was afraid when my time came to recite them that I would forget them. We had to name them all at once, one right behind the other. One of the boys in the class asked to be excused but the teacher wouldn't let him. Someone noticed "water running under their desks" and told the teacher. The boy had wet in the floor because he couldn't hold it any longer. We thought it was really exciting.

# Mill Whistle

People who lived in town had their own built in alarm clock. The mill whistle always blew every morning at 5:30 a.m., 12 noon, and at 10 minutes to 1 p.m. as a warning to get ready to go back to work and at one o'clock to go back to work. It blew again in the afternoon for work to be over at 3:30 p.m. My Dad always got up by the mill whistle until he died at age 88.

# Easter

The twins always got the works for Easter. A new dress, a pocketbook, gloves, frilly socks, and patent shoes. Of course, the Easter basket was filled with goodies. We got one even if no one else in the family got one. We were the youngest in the family so I don't remember the older ones at Easter. This just stood out in my mind because I would hear them whispering about it as to whether it would fit and if we would like it. A neighbor of ours also got into it as she didn't have any children and it gave her pleasure, I guess. She was a nurse and was really taken with the twins. We always went to church each Sunday. The church could be seen from our front porch it was so close to our home. About 3 minutes walking distance.

# My Mom's Sewing Machine

We weren't allowed to touch our Mom's sewing machine. We might break it or get our fingers caught by a needle. It was a pedal sewing machine. By that—I mean to get it to sew—you had to pedal it the whole time you sewed or it would not sew a stitch. No electric sewing machines then. It was kind of like patting your head and rubbing a circle on your stomach at the same time. You remember doing that as a child? My Mom made us a white pleated skirt using the sewing machine. She had to make two since we were twins. We needed it to be in the chorus at school. We wore white short sleeved sweaters with it and white shoes and socks.

# Bee

In the summer we didn't get many new shoes as children. We usually went barefoot as soon as it got warm enough. We just continued to wear our school shoes and they were usually well worn. The soles of our shoes would wear out first and we would put pieces of cardboard in the bottom of them. They would wear out in a circle about 2-3 inches in diameter. You could tell they were wearing out as you could feel the ground through the weak area—before it would break through. Leather shoes were hard to get because of the war.

To get on with my story—I was in the yard one day standing in the grass looking toward the mill and town when I stepped on a bee. It stung the heck out of the bottom of my foot right through that little hole in my shoe. It was safer to go barefoot as you at least see the sucker and not step on it. This was right after World War II and rubber was also hard to get for soles of your shoes.

# Sunbath

As a young teen I wanted to look my best so I tried to get a tan. I lay out in the sun in our front yard on a big towel and wore my bathing suit. It felt so good that I just kept laying a little longer. One day I stayed out nearly all day. Boy—did I pay for that!!! I didn't try that again. I got so sunburned I was miserable and of course I peeled which didn't help any. There went looking my best for a while. Not to mention I was blistered.

# First Silk Panties

One day my mom went shopping and when she came home she handed me a bag. In it was six pair of panties. They were all made of cotton except one pair. It was made from silk. We had always worn cotton panties before so of course, I took the silk panties for myself. Boy did they feel good on your skin. They felt so good!!! They felt so cool, especially since it was summer time. I guess you can say that was my first grown-up panties. Or at least they made me feel that way.

# Pen Pals

I had several pen pals when I was a young girl. They were all boys, of course. I wrote to them for several years. If their letters got boring I would stop writing them and start writing to another one. I can't remember where I got the addresses from. One boy I wrote got his brothers to writing to me also. When they got too serious I would stop writing them. They would want to come to see me and I knew my parents would not stand for that. I just wanted a Pen-Pal.

# World War II

World War II happened when I was in my early teens. All of my brothers went to war. It played havoc on the older brother's marriages. At the same time it nourished another. "Buzz" was stationed in South Carolina and that was where he met his wife-to-be. They were in close contact so their romance flourished.

My older brother, Wallace, was on a ship most of the time only coming into New York harbor to reload and depart again. He only got to come home a couple of times in three years. His wife would meet him when the ship docked for a few days. My Mom met him there one time with his wife.

Roy was stationed in Florida and things were so expensive there he couldn't afford for his wife to live there. So both marriages suffered and they later divorced. They both remarried and each had a daughter.

# Army Nurse Corps

During World War II the Army Nurse Corp was activated. My sisters, Annie Dee and Winnie had to join as they were in

Nurses' training in Tennessee. If needed they would have been called to nurse the sick and wounded soldiers. As it was, they weren't called to active duty. After the war they were given the option to stay in the Army or be discharged. Annie Dee chose to stay in while Winnie came out. Annie Dee stayed in and retired from the Army with a high rank.

# Transportation

As a result of World War II, transportation was hard to come by—there were few cars. If we wanted to go somewhere, we walked to town and caught the city bus. If we wanted to go to West Canton, North Canton, Smathers Hill or North Hominy we had to go by city bus as it was too far to walk. If we went to Waynesville or Asheville we caught a Trailways Bus or the train. The city bus came to the terminal every couple of hours. The city bus stop was in front of Sluder's Furniture Company that was across from the Post Office on Main Street. It would pick you up there but you would still have to walk some distance to where you were going. I remember going with my Mom to Balsam on the train to visit my grandparents. We had to walk down a road to get to their house.

# Rationing

During World War II several things were rationed. Among them were gas, sugar and coffee. Each family was issued a stamp book with the amount for the family. As you bought and paid for the item a stamp was torn out of your book. When it was empty you couldn't get anymore until time for the next book. Tires for cars and bicycles were hard to come by. Second-hand ones were used a lot. The auto makers were making tanks and items for use in the war. Car making was at a standstill. That in turn made it difficult to get a car and if you did it was an old one. It took a few years after the war for production to increase and get back to normal.

# Iron

Remembering how we used to iron in the early 30's brings to mind an incident that happened one cold winter morning. I had gotten up and went straight to the kitchen where it was warm. I was standing looking at the stove and there on the stove was the old iron kettle with steam coming out of it. Close by the kettle was a couple of cast irons. They stayed on the stove all the time. They were used to iron clothes. They were also used on cold nights to wrap in a thick cloth and put in our beds at the foot to keep us warm.

My Mom was cooking oatmeal for our breakfast. I started to pass out. I don't know why as I did it a lot as a child. My Mom caught me before I could fall on the stove. I was put back to bed and stayed home from school. Probably just a childhood disease as I caught them all. Electric irons came along a little later.

# After School

There were three drugstores in town that had a soda fountain and there was one without a soda fountain. After school we always walked home as town students didn't ride the bus. They were reserved for children outside the city limits. We walked to and from school come rain or shine. We always stopped at one of the drugstores for refreshments. A coke or ice cream always hit the spot. The places would be packed and noisy.

*Hendrix's Drugstore is behind the striped awnings.*

There was an ice cream parlor but it usually wasn't open until later. It usually stayed open until around 11 o'clock but the drugstores closed earlier—about 9 o'clock. Walking to school had its advantages. Country folks had to ride the bus to and from school therefore having to go straight home.

The drugstore finally closed their fountains as there was so much noise and some of the older customers complained about the noise. They were there to pick up their prescriptions and we would have all the seats and they couldn't sit down to wait for the medicine to be filled. The drugstores each in turn closed their soda fountains and as far as I am concerned that killed the drugstore. They were there for us during our high school years, however.

# Studying

In high school we always had home work, usually just to study or read. I always carried my books home but I never opened them. Not one time! I had no where to study at home. We had no desk in a quiet area to study in. Our dad would turn off the lights at 7:00 p.m. and we had to go to bed or sit up with the lights out. I might add—there were no night lights in our rooms either. We weren't afraid of the dark. Of course, there was a street light that shined all night into the house. It didn't bother our sleep either as we were used to them.

Back to studying—I usually studied in study hall at school. I passed my subjects and never worried about passing. But I will admit that I wasn't an "A" student. I would have fainted if I would have made an "A". The only "A" I ever made was in the first quarter in "Nursing". I don't remember being great at spelling but I must have learned something as I am a good speller today. Parents make a big mistake by not having a study area for their children—in an area where it's quiet away from everyone and especially away from the television.

# Fish Day

Every Friday our dad brought home fresh fish for supper. He would bring white fish and oysters. I liked the white fish and

Tommie liked the oysters. I couldn't stand to look at oysters, let alone eat them. They looked like "green chicken manure" in the center to me. He always brought plenty as it made a big platter full.

# Mowing

My brother, Buzz, used to mow yards for the whole neighborhood. He would come home wet with sweat. He didn't care as he was proud of himself for earning some spending money. Everyone was good to him and gave him cold lemonade to drink when it got hot.

He also worked as a mailman when he got older. He walked and delivered the mail to people's door all over town. He did that one summer about a year before he graduated from high school. He walked all over our side of town for about four hours everyday as it took him that long to cover the territory. Again people would have him something cold to drink as it got pretty hot in July. He had one leg shorter than the other as the result of a broken leg when he fell down our front concrete steps as a child.

# Pony

Ironic as it may seem—both the doctor's sons in our community had a pony. They were kept in a pasture somewhere else out of town. They brought them to our street to ride occasionally. I wanted to ride one time and they were going to let me. I tried to get on and every time I would just about get up my nerve and almost be upon it they would make the pony kneel and make me slide off. I never did really get to ride either one of them. Leave it to a little mean boy to be cute. I really wanted to ride that pony.

The doctor whose son I babysitted had a recording machine he would record his daughter when she cried as a baby. He recorded his children's first words and then later when they learned to talk. This was before tape recorders or camcorders as we know them today. He also took moving pictures of them playing with us. They would show them to us on a white screen on the wall. They were like moving pictures screens that were used in the schools. We call them audios. He took pictures one day when he had the pony out and he was riding in the street in front of our house.

# Snow And Snow Cream

During the winter we had snow frequently. We always made the most of it. We sleighed to our hearts content. I remember we had but one pair of rubber goloshes (overshoes). Whoever got them first got to wear them all day. They kept your feet dryer than the socks we put over our shoes to keep the snow out of our shoes. The goloshes had belonged to an older sister who had outgrown them.

When it snowed we always made snow cream. We would fill a bowl with clean white fluffy newly fallen snow. To this we put sugar over the top like you would sugar a bowl of cereal. We picked the richest milk we could find and poured it into the snow with the sugar and stirred it until it was mushy. We then added vanilla to make it taste like vanilla ice cream. It never gave us the sore throat. We ate it to our hearts content. We always used the first day's snow—never if it was discolored with sediment from the mill. That's why we always got it as soon as it fell.

*The Cemetery where the Jones are buried.*

# Grandpa Jones

My grandpa Jones died in the winter of 1949-1950. I went to the funeral with my mom. I was the only grandchild still living in the area. All the rest were off in school or were working. I remember standing in the snow on a hill when he was being buried. It was cold and windy. He was buried in Waynesville, N. C. He died from pneumonia and old age. He was 72. He just got sick and went to the hospital and never came home. He died there. After Grandma Jones died he used to catch the bus and come and stay with

*Grandpa Jones with grandchild, William Henderson Jones.*

us sometimes for a few days. My daddy didn't like it much because he chewed tobacco and he didn't like his spitting.

# Strangers

Warning children to avoid strangers is nothing new. As a child I was cautioned to never take a ride with anyone no matter if I knew them or not. One such day I had been to play with a girl who lived across town. On the way home a car slowed down by me and told me to "get in." He said, "I'll take you home." I said, "No" as I had been told. I told him that I would just walk. I was almost home anyway. Well, this man kept following me and asking me to get in. I kept refusing. He laughed and said "I'm on my way to see your daddy. I'm going right to your house. Come on and ride." I still stood my ground and didn't ride with him. Guess what?? When I got home there he sat on the porch with my dad. He had gotten there before me. He laughed and told my dad that he had trained me well and I wouldn't trust him to bring me home. He was a friend of my brothers as well as my dad. We were cautioned many times about accepting rides. I just did as I was told. I really wanted to ride but I knew my parents wouldn't let me go to play across town again if I didn't mind.

*Above: The "Treasure Chest" that was in Winnie's room. Right: A wooden Kewpie Doll.*

# Hidden Treasures

My two older sisters were gone from home at the same time when they were taking Nurses Training in Tennessee. They left some of their clothes and belongings at home. A chest of drawers with two long drawers and two short drawers was in Winnie's room. The bottom drawer could be locked. Well—curious as children are, my twin and I discovered we could take out the drawer above the bottom one which was the locked one to get to the "goodies" in the drawer below. We'd play with Winnie's doll and wear her sweaters to school. The doll was a "Kewpie" doll made of wood. It's arms and legs were jointed. It's head was round and had yellow hair painted on it to look curly. I guess you would call it a molded head. When we heard our parents talking about the sisters coming home we scampered to get those things back in the drawer as near as we could like they were. We were on pins and needles until they left. If they noticed that we had been in the drawer it was never mentioned or anything said about it.

# Vacation

One summer my brother, Roy, was taking my Mom to visit her sister in Virginia. Everything was fine until time for them to leave. We didn't know who got to go until they started getting in the car. It seemed that everyone got to go but Winnie, Daddy and us the twins. Well, Tommie and I started begging to go with them. The answer was clear—there was no room for us. The car was packed with someone at every window. As the car started to move Tommie and I grabbed the door handle and would not turn it loose. We were crying all the time "We want to go too!!" You could tell that they felt sorry for us but that didn't help our feeling of being left out. This went on every time they would get our hands loose—we would grab the door handle again and crying our little hearts out.

My mom got out and tried to console us, then a brother tried, but to no avail. Finally Daddy and Winnie had to hold us each bodily. We were kicking, screaming, and crying and our faces were wet with our tears. Our noses were running from our crying. They finally got a quick get away while we were being held.

Winnie took us into the house and we were still whimpering like little pups. She announced that we had a whole box of candy that was left for all who didn't get to go to Virginia. That saved the day for them as we did like candy. In a few minutes we had forgotten all about Virginia.

# Summertime Snacks

As you know children are always hungry. We earned money by babysitting. At night our parents always went to bed early as my dad had to get up early to go to work. In the summertime you just don't want to go to bed at least until it got dark. They would think we were in bed also. Well—we weren't! We would wait until we thought they

*My parents room beyond the wall on the left side of the stairs.*

were asleep then we would take turns sneaking down the stairs and out the front door to town. We always would get a pint of ice cream for each of us and a funny book each. We would swap after we read ours. We would also get a different flavor of ice cream each time. Yes—we ate a pint of ice cream each!!! We would buy our goodies and then sneak back up the stairs so softly because the stairs were right over our parents bedroom. Those stairs got a work out in the summer. If they heard us our dad would call out and scare the daylights out of us "all right get in bed"! We only did this when we weren't playing hide and seek with the neighbor kids.

# First Bedroom

O ur upstairs consisted of two average size rooms and a small one half size of a smaller room. Well—my older sister, Dee, got the one half room because it looked out over the town and the mill. The air circulated better there in the summer time also. Anyone knows how hot an upstairs can get in July and August. We would stay up until it cooled down some. Midday was almost impossible to stay up

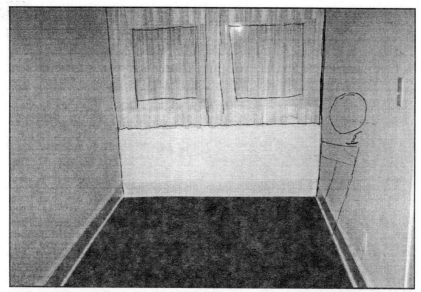

*Make believe you see a half bed on the left side of the room. To the right was a dresser that I had a mirror behind. The candle sat on the dresser on the right side, away from the curtain. You could see the town out the windows. It was a great view.*

there for over a few minutes at a time. There were no air conditioners for us to use. Even a fan didn't help much.

After Dee left home for Nurse's training, I captured the one-half room for mine. Since it had no electric outlets, I was pushed to use a candle so I could see in the mirror to comb my hair and experiment with cosmetics. I hoarded those candles as if they were precious gold. I was so proud of my independence as a pre-teen. The room was only big enough to hold a half bed but to me it was the same as a big bed. I was all to myself with no one else having to sleep with me. With so many children we had to sleep more than one to a bed when we were smaller.

# Mama's Flowers

My mother loved flowers. She kept them in pots on our front porch railing in the summer. In the winter we had to carry them inside. I hated it because we would get dirt on our hands and they crowded our house in the winter. Of course, it was our job. The kids had to carry while she directed where they were to go. After I married and left home she had a room built off the kitchen she especially made for her flowers. She had window seats made in front of the windows to set the pots on. This kept them off of the floor and more organized. I sure wish she had gotten the idea sooner. She would trade plants with friends.

She also had an outdoor assortment of unusual flowers that she tended regularly. The violets that come up in the spring had the sweetest smell. They smelled so sweet you almost wanted to eat them. The Women's Flower Club members used to come to her house when they needed a certain flower they couldn't find. She almost always had them. After she died my dad kept a flower of hers alive until he died eight years later. Now we all have a pot of flowers from that very same plant, we have kept alive, and my mom has been dead since 1968.

# Paper Dolls

On rainy days in the summer or on cold days in the winter when we couldn't go outside to play, Tommie and I would play with paper dolls. We would make a doll house on the table, that had different rooms. We played as though we were a family. We had a mom, dad, and little children. The paper dolls were punched out of a book we bought at the 5 and 10 cents store. We would play for hours on end. They would get up and eat breakfast, go to work or school just like a real family. They had names we gave them. Their clothes stayed on them by little flaps at the top of the dress or shirt. You just folded them down and the clothes stayed on. Of course, we had to hold the doll to play so that the clothes stayed on. No Barbies then.

# Play House

Having a twin, gave us a playmate, which I am sure helped our parents. That way we stayed out of their hair. We would make a playhouse outside using rocks and pieces of coal to outline the room. We would use big rocks or a brick for chairs and furniture. We would play there all day sometimes. We had a big doll that was made of cotton for the body. The head, legs, and arms were made out of some hard material. We could hold the doll by the arm and make it walk beside us. It's legs would move forward when you moved the doll from side to side.

We took movie star names as ours. Mine was Veronica Lake and my husband was Sterling Hayward. Tommie's husband was Tyrone Power. I don't remember who she pretended to be. We never lacked for something to do.

# Reservoir Hill

As we got older and went to high school we acquired new friends that lived across town from us and nearer the school. On Sunday we used to visit and we would walk around town. One day we decided to climb the hill to the Canton Reservoir. When we got up there we climbed upon the big concrete structure and looked out all over Canton. It was a magnificent view. The reservoir was a big round concrete structure with a concrete top on it. We didn't see any water.

# Parties

These friends also liked to have parties on Friday night. They would be held at their homes and all kids in the community came. Just good clean fun—no drinking. We played "spin the bottle" and all the usual kissing games. This introduced us to kissing and boys. How shy some of the kids were. Sometimes a boy would walk us home.

# North Canton - Reservoir Hill

Now this reservoir was on a high hill also but worse. The reservoir was also an open pool with a wire fence around it. You could throw things in it if you chose. I had been warned to not go near them as they could suck you under. I heeded their advice. I believe someone drowned there in later years. The party got kind of rowdy as they were smoking and couples were pairing off—so we left after a while. We had cooked hot dogs over an open fire and toasted marshmallows. So all in all it was a good picnic.

# Washing Car

When Wallace got old enough to get a job, he bought a car. About once a week in the summer, he would take it up the river above the high school to wash it. Tommie and I like to tag along. There weren't any car washes at the time. They came later. He would pull the car out into the river where the water came up to the top of the tires. He would soap and rub it good first. Tommie and I would be wading and playing in the water. After he got it rubbed down good with soap, he would rinse it with clear water. He used a bucket to throw water on it. W couldn't help him as we would probably throw it on each other as well, accidentally of course. Soap suds would float down the river. One day we sighted a water snake on an old tree limb in the water. We threw rocks we got from the river bottom at it. It finally sailed into the water and went on downstream. I was afraid it might swim toward us. I was ready to get the heck out of its way. I always looked for a snake after that when I went with him and I stayed close to him and the car. I was still just a little girl.

# Rabbit Tobacco

Children have to try everything. We were no exception. As we noticed our older brother and sisters and older playmates trying things we decided we would too. One such experiment was smoking rabbit tobacco. We hid so no one would catch us. It really didn't "smoke" all that good. But we did have fun trying, anyway. I never really took up smoking as I just didn't get anything out of it. I had rather eat candy. It didn't "smoke" I guess as we pulled it green and rolled it in cigarette paper we had "snitched". All that probably burned was the paper it was wrapped in. So much for that.

# My Dad's Pipe

Anyone who knew my dad will remember him and his pipe. If he was up that pipe was in his mouth. Some of the time it didn't even have tobacco in it. He would keep the pipe in his mouth even though the tobacco was all smoked up in it. It must have been his security blanket. He smoked Sir Walter Raleigh tobacco that he bought in a big can. When the pipe wasn't in his mouth, it was on a table by his easy chair. It would lay in a pipe holder that my older sister sent to him when she was overseas in the service. When filling the pipe he would spill tobacco and there were always bits of tobacco laying on the table by the pipe holder. He kept his tobacco in a leather pouch and it was difficult to get the tobacco out without spilling some of it. Sometimes he would clean it by scraping it out with his pocket knife. I never saw him with a cigarette. Occasionally he smoked a cigar, if someone gave him one.

*My Dad's Pipe*

# Seventh Grade

There was a teacher that a couple of girls and I decided we didn't particularly like. She had pets and favored them and ignored us. So we made up that we weren't going to study in her class. We didn't realize that we were the ones to suffer, not her. Well—guess what? We all three failed! One of them was not my twin sister. The principal didn't want to separate us so they failed Tommie too. We both had to repeat the seventh grade. All our other school friends got to go to Jr. High and we were left behind in grammar school for another year. You see, this little plot of ours, not to pass wasn't thought out beforehand. The other girls' parents sent them to summer school. Because there were two of us to go our parents decided we could just repeat the grade. Of course, Tommie made all A's the second year and was the smartest student in the class. I studied that year. I had learned my lesson.

# President Franklin Roosevelt In Canton

A big event happened in 1940. President Franklin Roosevelt came through Canton in a motorcade. He was here to dedicate the Parkway. I stood on the corner by Belk's Department store. The motorcade came from Asheville so they came down the hill from our then Fire Department and proceeded between Belk's and the drugstore and on down Park Street. He was in an open car with the top down. He waved as he went by. It happened so fast. He was there one minute and gone the next. It gave me an euphoric feeling. I was seeing a part of history. Really a historic minute in my small life. I was only eleven years old at the time. I was so close to the car that if it had stopped, I could have touched it.

# Beer Joints

There were several beer joints in town when I was growing up. The elite as well as the poor frequented them. The church people, of which I believe the First Baptist Church was definitely one, decided to do something about them. They also gambled with "ball tickets" from these beer joints. It was just a regular hangout. I want to say that petitions were taken around and signed to get them removed. My mom took a big part in it as she hated the bad habit of drinking alcohol. The town went "dry" in 1946. I am pretty sure that one beer joint was closed before this.

# Sex Education

In the seventh grade the girls got to talking about the "birds and the bees." There were little pamphlets that we read. No sex education in the school until in high school. We were shown a film that we were warned to be quiet and not laugh. We were all as quiet as a mouse during the movie and the rest of the day. I mention this because of the extensive controversy today about sex education. That was the extent of my sex education.

# Cold Bathroom

Heating a house was a problem in the 1930's. Sometimes some of the rooms were cold as the heat couldn't get to them. Our bathroom was one of those rooms. In the summer it was all right but in the winter it was a problem. However, we didn't let it bother us. We took a bath in the tub without any heat in the room. You could see your breath before your face, it was so cold. I found that steam from the hot water took the chill off of the room. So I would run the hot water first and then cool it down with cold water. It didn't take much as the tub was cold before water was put into it.

The hot water came from a tank behind our cook stove that was kept hot by the fire being in the stove. When the fire went out the water would get cold. This tank only held about 30 gallons, so when it was used the next person had to wait for it to reheat. Very few baths were taken early in the day. We used this water from the tank also to wash dishes.

I took many "mini" baths. This is a bath taken while standing up and washing with a wash cloth with water from the wash basin. The hot water went further this way. I washed this way every morning whether I had taken a bath the night before or not. Electric water heaters weren't available yet.

# Broom Stick Skirts

Broom stick skirts were a craze when I was a teenager. It was a full skirt that was gathered at the waist and the length was to the knee or a little below. There were simple to make. You took about three yards of material, according to how full you wanted it to be. You gathered it at the top and hemmed the bottom. You sewed it up the side and then put a waist band on it and a placket at the side. No zippers were used. You measured the waist with a piece of cloth for size and then sewed in on the skirt making a waist band and the last touch was a button hole sewed by hand and a button. The whole project was sewed by hand. The material costs about $2.00. When I wanted a new skirt, I just went to town and bought my material and one time made a skirt one night and wore it to school the next day.

# Visiting

There was and still is a row of houses bordering the Locust Field Cemetery behind the Pennsylvania Avenue School (now the new Library). Families of black people lived in them. One day my mom went to visit a lady who lived in one of them. She let me go with her. I had never been close to a black person, so it was a new experience for me. I was just a child. When we got there, the colored lady was on the porch in a chair. She wore a dress and an apron. She was about my Mom's age and size. We stayed on the porch for a while and for some reason Mom and the lady got up and went inside the house. They told me to come in too. I was reluctant to do so as I was just a little bit afraid of her because of her color. She was different from us and in my child's mind I was scared of her. When my mom went in the house with her I was a little bit apprehensive and looked through the screen door to be sure that she was all right. I felt scared there on the porch alone. I kept looking to see if anyone else was coming as I was prepared to run if there was.

The First Baptist Church of Canton helped the Negro people get their church organized. Our minister helped their preacher on how to preach instead of just reading from the Bible. The women also helped with getting a Women's Missionary Society started. This might have been why my mom was there. This is the time that Negroes had their own school and church. It was before desegregation.

# Old Graves

While I was still going to grammar school at Pennsylvania Avenue, a new auditorium was added to the existing building. To do this, they had to dig up some graves and move the coffins to another place. Tales went around that some of the lids were opened and the remains looked at. They told that the coffin of one was full of hair as the hair had continued to grow after the person was buried. The hair was supposed to be all around the body, all the way to its feet and back up the side. They also told that the fingernails were like claws about three inches long and curled under. As children we believed all this. I am sure it was just scary tales. I don't know who the graves belonged to or where they were taken to. It does give food for thought as I doubt that anyone was embalmed back then.

# Dog Days

In the hot days of summer we were warned about "mad dogs". It would be hot and dry for a long period of time. This was supposed to be when dog's went "mad". If our mom went to town or left the house for very long, she would lock us in the house. If we wanted to play outside, it had to be close to the house. It used to really scare me as I would look out the windows or the screen door to see if I could see one. We were told that they would foam at the mouth and stagger. I never did see one but the memory of it lingers. We were told that they would attack us and bite us and then we would get the disease and it would kill us as there was no cure. You rarely hear of "dog days" anymore.

# Flipping

There was a craze going around of slipping up behind some one and flipping them with your fingers. Really, just a quick "smack", only you used just your fingers. It hurt like crazy for just a minute and really no harm done. One day I walked into the kitchen and my Mama was standing in front of the sink with her back to me. The temptation was too good. I slipped up behind her and "flipped" her on the buttocks. Boy, did she react fast. She whirled around and grabbed for me. It surprised me so, I started running. She was right behind me as I ran out the door and down the walk heading to the street. I jumped those steps two at a time until I got to the bottom in the road. She was right behind me but she stopped at the top of the steps shaking her hand at me and telling me not to do that again. That was the fastest I ever saw my mom move.

# Teacher Cruelty

In grammar school something happened that I can't forget. There was a boy in our class that I felt this teacher constantly picked on. She took him to the Principal's office for every little thing. I remember the teacher and the boy having an argument one time and she slapped him. I could never see what he had done wrong. It happened so fast. I feel she picked on him because he came from a poor family. Anyway, he never finished school. I wonder today if that punishment discouraged him from it. Of course, he shouldn't have talked back to her but it might have been handled another way.

# Cherokee Indian Fair

Every Fall my mother and her sister from Virginia went to Cherokee to the fair. It was their outing together every year. They caught the bus early in the morning and stayed all day. I have a tall wooden vase she brought home from there one time. The colors painted on it were all colors like a totem pole. The colors have faded but I still have the vase. She would have other trinkets and Indian corn still on the cob. Not having a car didn't keep my mom at home.

# Hay Fever

My mom took the hay fever in the fall of the year. It would make her eyes water continually and her head would stop up. Late in the evening is when it bothered her the most. She would make Tommie and me stay outside and she would close the door. She had a little dish that she would burn something in that was supposed to help the hay fever. I think it was sulfur. It sure did smell strong. The hay fever would make her have trouble breathing. She would hold her head over the dish and inhale the fumes. When they finally let us back in the house you could still smell it. I don't know why we had to stay outside unless she didn't want us smelling it or else so we wouldn't open the door until she was finished.

# III.

# North Hominy
# Haywood County
# 1950-1968

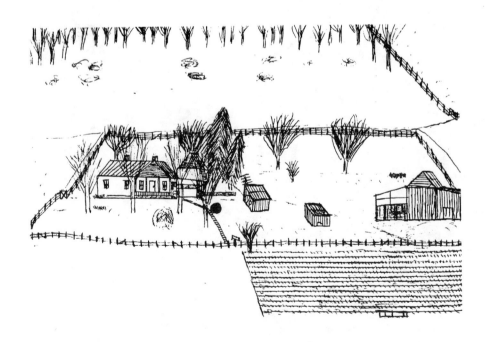

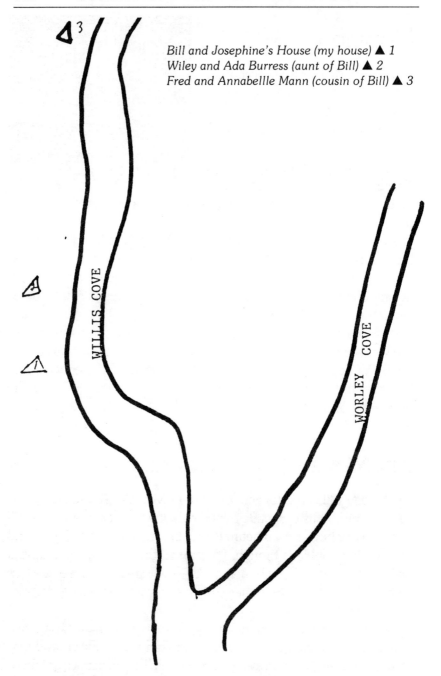

Bill and Josephine's House (my house) ▲ 1
Wiley and Ada Burress (aunt of Bill) ▲ 2
Fred and Annabellle Mann (cousin of Bill) ▲ 3

These are the houses that I could see from my house.

# Eloping

*Bill and Jody—1950*

M ost girls like a big wedding, but not me. I was never one for fanfare. I didn't care one bit to put on a show for anyone, especially with me the main attraction. We eloped to Greenville, South Carolina. I had written them ahead of time to ask their requirements and this eliminated a waiting period. No blood test was needed either.

We left at eight in the morning and were home by four-thirty in the afternoon. By the time we found the Court House, it was almost the lunch hour for the employees there. They asked us to come back at one o'clock. We went down the street and found a little diner where we had a sandwich.

After we got married and started home we got lost in Greenville. We went around and around before we finally found our way out of town. We kept the marriage a secret for a while. The marriage lasted 19 years until his death. Where or how you get married isn't any guarantee of its lasting.

# My Move To The Country

T he day Bill came for me to move in with him still stands out in my mind. His car made a loud racket when it came up the hill to get to our house. You heard it long before you saw it. The sound was unmistakably his though. He parked the car and came up the walk to the house. I met him at the door with my suitcase and a box with my few belongings in them. My mom was there but my dad was at work.

Going out that door changed my life forever. A new experience was waiting for me. His mother had taken the week off and was cleaning house. She had a lady there to help her. When we got there they had cooked lunch for us. I believe it was steak. They had taken the curtains down and were cleaning everything. She had moved her

*Wood house where Jo lived in the country.*

things from the master bedroom to a smaller one. She let us use her big bedroom. Bill had bought a bedroom set that included a bed, a dresser, and a chest of drawers. It was put in the room for us.

Wanting to help, I offered to do something. I was given the job of ironing—about six long sleeved white dress shirts of Bills. I was terrified that I would scorch one of them. We had to sprinkle clothes before we ironed them or we couldn't get the wrinkles out. No steam irons yet. I found they ironed easier if they were put in the refrigerator for a while to get cold. I learned this by accident. If the clothes were sprinkled and didn't get ironed that day they could mold. So we put them in the refrigerator and discovered they ironed better after being there.

After two years his mother moved to town to an apartment. They were put on different shifts and she had no way to work. Don't ever move your wife in with the mother-in-law!! No two women can live under the same roof. Living with your mother-in-law is not easy. For starters you are nervous enough getting used to being married, let alone trying to please your husband's mother. You see—I used to smoke—not much, but I did smoke one now and then. Well, the first week I lived there, I overheard her talking to someone on the telephone about what a great daughter-in-law she had. She was saying that I didn't smoke like her daughters. Well—I quit smoking completely as I had to live up to her expectations. I really didn't have time to anyway as there was always something to keep me busy.

I learned to milk the first week after I moved. A neighbor showed me how. We had to first climb the mountain to find the cow. She was on the very top of it. I made the mistake of learning to milk because it then became my job. I am afraid of cows, remember!!!

My first meal was a disaster. The mill changed shifts around so Bill and his mother weren't working the same shift anymore. This was my first meal to cook without Hattie being there. First—I didn't know how to get a wood stove hot enough to cook bread. I asked my husband how to make cornbread but he said he didn't know. I had watched his mother but I hadn't paid any attention how much salt, baking powder, and soda to put in it. You see—it was plain corn meal that had been ground from corn—not the self-rising kind we have today. She didn't measure the ingredients. It was a pinch of this and a pinch of that. It's so easy to make bread today even a child could do it.

Back to my meal—to begin with the stove wasn't hot enough and the bread just sogged and didn't cook. It was in the oven about two hours and was still not done. I found out later that my husband knew how to make bread. He just let on like he didn't for fun to see what I would do. He told his mother when he went in to work 3-11, and I later found it out. She had worked days that day. I had noticed he had kept looking at me from behind the paper he was supposed to be reading. My first meal cooked in the country was definitely a total

*Willis Cove: First house is the Wood house. The second house is the Wood Grandparents house. (Aunt Ada lived here.) The third house is the Mann house.*

disaster. I didn't have MacDonalds or Hardee's to go to. I was not allowed to bring sandwich bread into the house—according to him—it had too many preservatives in it.

I think being in the military might have helped form some of his opinions. He wouldn't eat anything he had eaten while in service. Some of his ideas would blow the minds of young girls today. Imagine having to cook with the thought in mind that part of it was going into a lunch bucket for all of his co-workers to see. So you can probably tell where I spent a lot of my time—in the kitchen or the garden. We only bought the essentials from the store. I hate packing a lunch to this day. I made sure when I remarried that there were no lunches to pack. It was just as bad as he came home to lunch everyday. A way to a man's heart is through his stomach, and I believe it. Men—can't live with them—can't live without them.

# Scared

The first week after I moved to the country Bill was working 3-11. His mother and him both worked in the same department at the mill. They worked in the Finishing room. Her job was to sort paper and his was to keep the women supplied with paper to sort. The week I moved, his mom had taken a week's vacation to get ready for me. She gave us her bedroom. At night she would read and I would embroider. She liked "Modern Romances".

One night we were each "doing our thing" while sitting in the living room. All of a sudden there came this sound from the front porch as if someone was on it. It sounded like someone shaking the screen door. The inside door was shut. I looked up and looked at her and she made no move to go to the door to see who or what it was. She didn't even let on that she had heard it. I continued to embroider and then the sound came again only louder. I looked up again and still she didn't let on. Well, it was scaring me. I couldn't understand why she was ignoring it. I then thought, well, it can't be much as she didn't seem alarmed.

A little later the door rattled again. This time she laid her book down and didn't say a word. She just went to the door and opened it. I was scared and stayed behind her. There on the porch was a stray dog that was scratching fleas. It was laying against the door and every time it scratched the door would shake. I learned that there is usually a reason for all sounds you hear. So I learned to live with them. She ran the dog off of the porch and it didn't come back. It was spooky as I was in a strange place and didn't know what to expect. I have learned now that house noises can be the wind making the boards creak and rodents making noises in the wall at night when they are out looking for food.

# My Neighbors In The Country

O ur nearest next door neighbor was Wiley and Ada Burris - Bill's aunt.

The next house was a cousin of Bill's. Fred and Annabelle Mann and his mother Aunt Daisy. If you screamed they could not hear you.

My only other neighbor was the trees, mountains, and the sky. I couldn't see a house at all unless I went out in the yard. Then I could only see two. From inside the house, I could see a beagle dog lying in front of it's house sleeping or a cow grazing in the pasture on the

*Our house sat on the right of the picture on the bank behind the telephone pole. The house has been torn down. Note the beautiful view!! The Creek is to the left between the field and the woods.*

*Left: You can see Ada's house in the background. John, Jim, and David in the snow. Note the bike. Right: Our yard with outbuildings. In the distance you can see Fred and Annabelle Mann's house.*

hill. It would occasionally throw its tail from side to side and then upon its back to knock off the flies that were constantly there. Flies are abundant where there are cattle. You could always tell when the cattle were close to the house because there would be more flies than usual to contend with. If the cattle were in the pasture away from the house we didn't have many.

# My Best Friend In The Country

Since I lived five miles from town, neighbors were sparse. My husband's aunt lived the closest to us so we became fast friends. She was about twenty years older than me but she took good care of herself and didn't look that old.

Her husband had TB that was in remission. He had to have B-12 injections for a period of time. Having been a doctor's assistant, I got elected to do the job. His wife bragged to his doctor that a nurse lived next door so I got to give the shots. I didn't know anything about B-12 shots but I gave them anyway. I was rewarded with a beautiful pearl and gold necklace with earrings to match that were bought at one of our better jewelry shops at the time. I was proud to wear them to church, mostly of how I had earned them.

This aunt, I am told, was something else before I knew her. She was always nice around me. I took her to church every Sunday with my children. I found later that people who knew her didn't think it would last. We went to church together for years and she had many friends there.

Every week we went to town together in her car. My husband had our car at work. She always did the driving and I could have walked faster than she drove. We never went all the way into town. You see, she couldn't park and was afraid of traffic. We never had an accident. We always went the back streets to find a parking place that we could just pull into. By the way, she always drove in the middle of the road.

I could always tell when a summer storm was coming as I'd look up and here she would come to my house. Always to the back door as I was always in the kitchen cooking or canning. She sat on her front porch and could see the clouds forming and then she would make a beeline to my house. She came on one occasion just barely ahead of the rain. She died just a short time after my husband. He had died a few years earlier. In less than five years I lost three people very close the me. The other besides her and my husband was my mother. No wonder I moved back to town.

# My Very First Country Bath

I had lived in the country about a week before I ventured to take a bath. For starters, the only bath facilities were an "out house" and if you wanted to take a bath, there was the wash tub that was set on the floor and filled with water. We heated the water on the wood stove in kettles. We also did this when we washed clothes as we didn't have water heaters.

In town we had a water heater that was connected to the back of the cook stove and as long as you had a fire, you had hot water. We didn't have this set up in the country. Today you see these old water heaters cut in half with flowers planted in them. I would say they are an antique.

Well—on this particular day—everyone was at work so I heated up the water and got the big wash tub. I put

*My country Bathtub—a big galvanized wash tub.*

it on the kitchen floor. To my dismay—there were no shades on the windows and there were four of them and they were all on ground level. I began to undress for the big event and all the time thinking "Boy, if my parents and family could only see how I had to take a bath." I kept looking at the windows to see if anyone was looking in. In town we always had a bathroom with a regular bath tub, commode, and wash basin and they were in the house. We also had shades on the windows. After about a year in the country, we had a bathroom put in the house. Everyone in the community came to see it—and was I glad for that day!!! The neighbors followed suit and put in a bathroom in their house. Out houses were soon a thing of the past.

# Fox Story

Ｎew mothers always have to handle new baby clothes and wash them before a baby comes. When I was pregnant with my first baby I was alone one afternoon so I proceeded to wash the new baby clothes. Of course, no dryer, so to the clothes line I go. I'm standing there hanging out clothes when this terrible racket startles me from behind. I turn around and about 20 chickens or rather banty chickens come flying out of the woods behind me. I am so surprised that I just stare—when low and behold out of the woods comes a fox. A beautiful red fox just stands there and stares at me and its not fifty

feet away. We out stare each other because we are both probably petrified unil it gave up and retreated back into the woods.

The house I lived in in the country was within sight of only two other houses. Notice I said sight—not sound. I couldn't even be heard shouting to the next house. These houses could only be seen if you were outside in the yard. To the back of the house was a hill with woods on it all the way to the top of the mountain. This was where the fox came from. To the front of the house was a road and then another pasture with more woodland. I guess you referred to the area as a cove that went to the end of the road. What I am trying to say is that the road ended above our house.

# Snakes

I had not lived in the country very long when one day my mother-in-law asked me to go to the hen house for the eggs. So off I go—well—I come to the garden that has grown up in weeds. I had to go through it to get to the hen house. I took one step into this wilderness and stopped dead in my tracks. There in front of me curled up in the grass is a snake. It was not a big snake but none the less it was a snake and I had never seen one before that was that close except in books. Well—you have heard of a snake scaring you stiff. That's exactly what it did to me. I froze in movement—with one foot on the ground and the other leg in mid-air—getting ready to put it down on the ground. I just stared at it for several minutes and it appeared to be looking back at me. I remember thinking how some people said how scared they were when they saw their first snake. Well—after getting my composure, I lowered my foot to the ground and turned and made fast tracks back to the house. I announced to my mother-in-law that I couldn't get the eggs because of the snake. I never went near that garden again or the chicken house until it was mowed and plowed and without so many high weeds. She said it was probably just a garden snake—but a snake is a snake to me.

Several years later we had a garden across the creek from the house. I either had to let the gate or "gap" down or else climb over the fence—so I chose to go over the fence. One time when going to the garden, I climbed over the fence near a pile of wood. When I was about half over the fence I looked and there laying on the wood was a snake sunning itself. My knees got kind of weak but I went on over the fence after just stopping for a moment. The snake didn't move.

My next challenge was the cows that I was so afraid of. So I got me a big stick (like it would help). The stick wasn't a bad idea but the size of it was what was unusual. I guess it was three or four times as long as I was tall. I mean it was a long sucker!! I hoped no one saw me because I looked so ridiculous with that long pole in front of me for protection. The cows were no where near me. In fact, they were at the other end of the pasture. I was sure my husband's relatives were looking at me and getting a good laugh at my expense. It was a Sunday and all the children came home on Sundays to eat lunch. I am sure someone was watching.

# Wood Stove

As a child I grew up in a house with a wood or coal stove to cook on and to keep warm. Most other people had electric stoves and a furnace. Well—in the country there was no choice but to use wood or coal.

When I first moved to the country I had to get up at four thirty in the morning to get the stove hot enough to bake bread. My husband

would not eat store bought bread. He believed the preservatives in it would give you cancer. I never had loaf bread from the store in my house for seven years until my children went to school and wanted a sandwich. My husband's lunch was packed from the table— no sandwiches for him. If I sent one he promptly brought them back home to me.

So I learned real fast after ex- perimenting a while what would get the stove hot quick. I started out gathering kindling from the woods—such as bark and rich pine. Rich pine is wood from a pine tree that is seasoned and very easy to burn and it gets very hot to the point of being dangerous. It can catch your house on fire if you use too big a piece. You usually use just a splinter to start a fire. I would take a burlap sack and go to the woods and gather dry bark and small sticks. I learned that corn cobs after corn is shelled off of it was good—and boy did old tar paper off of a house get a stove hot quickly. I'm glad those days are gone—but the memories remain. I could do it again if I had to. You just don't think about it, you just do it.

# Mishaps

A week before my first child was born—a nephew was born. Well—it seems that the parents had a small daughter—approximately two years old. She was brought out to stay with us while the mother was in the hospital with the new baby. The mother was my husband's sister. It had been decided that the child would stay with her grandmother when the new baby came.

It ended up being Bill and me taking care of her as she was working the graveyard shift when the baby came. She had to sleep during the day and work at night. When she was awake she usually went to the hospital to see her daughter. Then, they were kept in the hospital several days, not just overnight, as today.

One day the little girl was in the yard playing while I was cooking lunch. My husband was supposed to be watching her but he was reading the paper—so you know how that is!! We heard this loud crying and screaming at the barn. We ran to see a mad hen with little chickens and it was flogging her as she was trying to get away. She had tried to pick up a little chicken and the mother hen didn't like it. My husband jumped up from the chair and literally ran to the barn and swept the little girl right up into the air away from the hen. The hen could have done great harm to the child if she had gotten close to her eyes. She was pecking her all over. No blood appeared so she wasn't hurt but was as scared as we were.

Another scare we had—my oldest son was also about two—and was in the yard. This happened a couple of years after the above incident. He was there playing in the yard and the next thing we know he's gone. He's sighted in the field with a horse. He was standing under the horse's head looking up at it. There he stood in his diaper and barefoot. He had gotten across the road, through the pasture and across the creek of water to get to the horse. We had to move slow to get him away without the horse running over him— but we did. Goes to show you how fast a two year old can move.

# House Cleaning

My mother-in-law believed in working the old timey way. You wash on Monday, iron on Tuesday, clean the whole house on Saturday and rest on Sunday. I kind of resented this as I never had learned to work that way. We would get up early on Monday when she worked 3-11 and put the big tub on the stove and fill it with water to get it hot to wash with. We then poured it by buckets into the washing machine. We would hang the clothes out to dry on the lines. She would go into work and I would have to bring them in and fold them to be ironed or put away.

On Saturday, the house was cleaned from the top to the bottom. She at first gave me the job of dusting the venetian blinds. They had to be dusted one at a time. I hated that as it took awhile. Then the furniture had to be waxed and polished and then shined. The floors were mopped and waxed every Saturday. She used to do these chores with me and soon it got to be my job, also. Kind of like when I was showed how to milk a cow and the next thing I knew it was my job.

One Saturday she had worked the graveyard shift and was in the bed sleeping. So I mopped the floors and after they dried, I was on my knees on the floor putting paste wax on them. I heard someone enter and thought it was one of the boys so I yelled "Get off my floor!! Can't you see I am waxing?"

Was I surprised when I turned around to see Hattie, my mother-in-law standing there, looking kind of sheepish. She said kind of quiet, "I just wanted to go to the bathroom." She had to cross the living room floor to get to it. Do you know she went right on over it anyway! There was an outhouse she could have used until the floor was ready to walk on. I was a little embarrassed to have yelled at her like that but it really felt good to just be able to vent my anger at being made to do all the work. She lived there with us for about two years before she moved to town to be closer to her job. Her and Bill were on separate shifts and she didn't drive and had no way to work but to walk. I felt the work I did sort of paid for my keep, after all it was her house.

# Mill Lunches

I guess the thing I hated the most about living in the country was having to pack a lunch to be taken to the mill. Bill wouldn't eat in the cafeteria. He would not eat a sandwich as he would not eat loaf bread. The bread had to be baked fresh every day, either biscuits or cornbread. So I had to pack the lunch from the table from what I cooked that day. It was a pain when I had to fix one when he worked days. I'd have to pack it the night before from what I had cooked for supper. I got tired of packing those lunches. I was so glad when a day off came or when he had a weeks vacation.

He would tell me how the other men would watch to see what he had. They told him how lucky he was to have a good home-cooked meal to eat. He wouldn't eat spaghetti or a sandwich. If I sent them they came back not eaten. He got a lot of either ham or sausage biscuits when he worked days and a boiled egg, among other things. He liked pickled eggs made from beet pickle juice.

One time I made a chocolate up-side-down pudding cake. I put some in his lunch in a plastic container. It wasn't eaten and he said "don't put that in my lunch again, it looks like it has already been eaten and spit back out." Jim, my son, however liked them so well that he requested one for his birthday, one time. They were made without an egg and was a very economical cake. I always cooked from scratch, no cake mixes. Sometimes eggs would be scarce and I wasn't allowed to buy them. In the spring we had more eggs than we could eat but in the summer and winter we had very few. Hens lay eggs frequently in the spring but when the weather got hot they would slow down and in cold weather they didn't lay at all. Bill would eat this cake at home though with whipped cream—hard to please men!!!

I made lunches for nineteen years, everyday of work, five days a week, without fail. The food was cooked on a wood cook stove with the produce coming from my garden or in the winter time, it was from the can house. We didn't buy very much from town to eat as we grew our own. We ate very little red meat except the liver from a pig when we killed them. It was usually pork or chicken that we raised on the farm. I packed his lunch in a black metal lunch box in plastic containers. I even had a pie shaped one for pie wedges. He took milk in his thermos. He wore out one lunch box and had to buy another one. The first one rusted out.

# Bear Story

After moving to the country, if I went to town, I had to catch a bus. Cars were not as plentiful as they are today. Usually only one car to a family and it was used for transportation to work. You didn't get a driver's license as fast as teens do today.

I would have to walk a mile down a dirt road to a little church to wait for the bus. The buses ran every hour until 8:30 at night. That would be the last one for the day.

One morning I was going down the road to catch the bus to town when I saw something that was jet black and velvet-looking off the bank. It kept moving but I couldn't see anything but a big black blob. There was no evidence of a head or tail. It kept moving but I couldn't

make out what it was. I didn't know how far out in the country I was—and I began to wonder if maybe it could be a bear. If it was—it was a big sucker. I thought—well surely not—but it doesn't pay to be too careful. I was going to have to walk right by it and there wasn't a fence between us. If there had been one—I would have went on down the road. Anyway, I slowed my walk until I got closer and then finally I lost my nerve and turned around and started back home. I went back home with my heart in my mouth and disappointed about my trip to town.

I had not been home in over a week and I was getting homesick. My mother-in-law was at home and she asked me why I had came home. She said "I thought you were going to town." I told her there was something black down the road and it looked like a bear. We watched for a few minutes and the black thing moved a little. Then it moved again and started up the bank. When it turned around we could see its head and it was a black Angus cow. I had never seen a black cow before. I didn't even know there was such a thing as our cow in town was red. I don't know who it belonged to. My mother-in-law didn't laugh and she kept a straight face. I bet she thought I was a dumb bunny. At this point I was still afraid of cows—so if it had not been a bear, I still would have been afraid of it. As you have guessed, my trip was postponed as the bus had already run and I had missed it.

# Telephones

In the 1940's our telephones in town did not have a dial tone or a number to dial. When you picked up the receiver an operator would ask "number please?" They in turn connected you to your party. No one else was on the line. The party lines came later. In the country in the 50's you were on a party line with four other people.

There were no telephones when I first moved to Hominy. I lived there about a year before telephones were available. Each family was given a number of times the telephone rang at one time. Ours was to ring three times with a pause and then three more times and so on until someone answered it.

Everyone on the line could pick up and listen to your conversation. There was little privacy so you watched what you said about your neighbors. If it rang at night after 11 o'clock I would listen. You see—

there was a lady that was popular with the opposite sex and you could hear them talking and asking her out or to meet them someplace. Shortly, you would hear a car going by our house or her going down the road in her car.

My husband didn't like the telephone. He thought they were for carrying tales or else someone wanting something. If he was home and it rang, he would not let me answer it. He would say if it was important they would call back and if it wasn't—then they didn't need to call anyway. He was always at work when I listened at night. As I hardly ever saw anyone—I couldn't very easily spread gossip. It was just a way of entertaining myself. The lady was single and if she wanted to date it was her business.

# Rock Garden

The first spring that I was in the country, I got bored. I hadn't yet been introduced to the garden. I decided to make a flower garden. My mom always liked flowers so I thought I would give it a try. I planted flowers near the smoke house but I soon discovered that it would not work, as the dogs and chickens liked that place to sleep and sun themselves.

So I decided to go farther from the house. The garden spot where I had encountered my first snake had been plowed so the weeds were gone. I decided to make a rock garden below the chicken house out of the way. I cleared the ground of twigs and rocks. I then proceeded to cut the brush and weeds. Some of them were tough and stubborn. So I had to pull them loose to get them out. Of course, I didn't wear gloves.

The next day I noticed my hands started to itch. I continued to work on my garden anyway. I had put on my shorts as it had gotten hot. The next day my legs started to itch also. Well, that night I woke up in total misery. My hands itched and my legs itched even worse. I clawed and scratched.

Then I remember someone saying that SO-Hy was good for poison ivy. I just happened to have some so I got up and wet my hands and legs good with the SO-Hy. I went back to bed thinking my misery was over. Was I surprised!! My legs started burning something awful. I was in total misery sure enough. That So-Hy was burning the living daylights out of me. I didn't sleep another wink all night. Don't use So-Hy on poison ivy especially if you have scratched and broken the skin. As you have guessed, the rock garden didn't get completed.

# Whistling in the Dark

I n the late 40's to early 50's we traveled by city buses. Cars were few and far between. You either walked or caught the bus. I had to walk a mile from the house to the bus stop. It stopped and turned around at a little white church.

I had been to town and had missed an earlier bus and it was dark when I got home. I was a little scared as it was really a black night. See—no street lights and no moon to see by. I started up the road with my purchases and walking as best I could to stay in the road. I visualized horses coming at me in the dark or a cow that may be out of the pasture.

I had gone a short distance when I heard a whistle from the other side of the road and it seemed to come from the pasture. Then I heard a whistle from the other side of the road. I stopped and listened

*The church where Jo caught the bus.*

and the whistle came again from where I had first heard it. It was as though someone was answering someone else. It would be on first the left side of the road and then on the right hand side. I didn't know what to do and I'll admit I was scared.

All of a sudden the worst yelling and running footsteps could be heard—then laughter. I stood petrified in the road. I didn't know whether to run or stand still. Then my name was spoken "Jody, is that you?" My mother-in-law had become concerned when I wasn't home before dark so she had sent my husband and a friend of his to meet me to walk me home. They decided to have a little fun out of it never dreaming they were going to scare the wits out of me. Well—they did!! From then on I was on the early bus, no more after dark buses for me.

# A Lesson Learned

After I married we moved in with Bill's mother. Before the first year was up I noticed they argued a lot. It seemed to me he couldn't do anything to please her. Every time he came home she would jump him about something. I got it in my head that she didn't like us living there . He felt like it belonged to him as much as her because his Dad had left it to them.

One day I wrapped up my baby, John, and caught the bus and went to town. I went to my parents for advice. I told them that I thought us being there with his mom was causing problems—I felt a little in the way. It was making life a little difficult for me. Well, my parents got real quiet. Finally they left the room.

When they returned they told me I had to live where my husband provided. They said I was to stay out of it and out of the way. I got my baby and walked back to the bus. Of course, my feelings were hurt so I cried and cried all the way to the bus. I made up my mind that I would stick it out and I did. If we would be a little firmer with our children today they would probably be less divorces. It made me a stronger person and determined to succeed.

# Tricked—Mischevious Deeds— Blackberry Picking

I had lived in the country a few months when one early summer day, Bill decided he was going to take me blackberry picking. We got up early one morning, that he was off from work, and off we went with our buckets. We walked up the hill and he led me through a pine thicket with heavy vines and limbs to block our way. We had to walk bent over because of the limbs on the pine trees being so close to the ground. The limbs pulled at my hair and clothes. On we went!! We finally got through it when I was about to be discouraged with the whole thing. I could barely stand up straight, I had been bent over so long and did my back hurt!! It felt like it was broken.

What was so bad—we still had to pick the blackberries. We picked our buckets full, all the time being on the lookout for snakes in the bushes. That really made my day, as I was terrified of a snake. My hands were blue from the juice from the berries. We walked back down the road to the house, me not suspecting at all that we could have gone that way in the first place instead of the pine thicket.

When we got home, his mother asked him how he took me to the blackberry patch. She said surely you didn't take her the way you left here—through the woods? He just grinned and said I needed the experience. The road paralleled the pine thicket and we could have walked up the road, instead of practically crawling on our hands and knees for about an hour. It would have taken about five minutes by way of the road.

You can better believe I didn't go berry picking anymore. If we had berries, he picked them or he had the children help him, when they got old enough. He was good for pulling pranks on you. He picked them and I canned them. I canned about 90 quarts one year. His reason being—there may not be any next year. He picked in the morning before he went to work 3-11 and I canned while he was at work.

I don't like blackberries very well to this day, as there were blackberries to can for weeks it seemed. It always started the canning season for me. Next would come kraut made from our home grown cabbage. I was always left something to do while he worked. I could not make a choice of my own what I wanted to do as there was always something necessary to be done to run a farm. No lounging at the pool for me.

# Dry Well

The summer I was pregnant with Cindy, my daughter, a house was being built up the road from our house. The day they drilled their well ours went dry. They must have hit our water vein.

The water level was so low in our well that the pump couldn't pick it up. The only way I could get water was to drop a bucket into the well and draw the bucket back up full of water. I used this water to cook with and to drink. If I needed to wash clothes or take a bath, I would have to carry water from the 'branch' and heat it on the stove. Think it over—I have two small boys and am pregnant and have to carry water to wash my hair, even, from the branch. Talk about keeping busy. No spare time for me.

I finally had the laundry in town pick up my clothes and sheets and they would wash them and bring them back to me wet and I would hang them out to dry. After Cindy was born I had a diaper service out of Asheville. They delivered me four dozen diapers twice a week. I used this service until she started wearing training pants. There were no disposable diapers then. Bill and a friend finally dug our well deeper and we had water again. Makes you learn to appreciate having water.

# Gathering Wood

For some reason, if it snowed or got really cold, Bill would have the older boys out gathering wood. It used to really upset me. Why wait until the ground is covered in snow to get the wood you know you are going to need? Why not get it in the Fall when it's still warm?

Anyway, I can still see those boys now with their boots and toboggans, gloves and coats on with water running down their face from the cold. I felt so bad for them, but I knew better than to interfere. I't didn't hurt them as they rarely ever had a cold. His thinking was "it'll make them tough".

# First Turkey

The very first time I ever cooked a turkey was after I married and moved to the country. You might say it was the first Thanksgiving for me to prepare. I had no idea how long to cook a turkey. I didn't even have a roasting pan or even a pan big enough to hold a turkey. The biggest thing I had that it would fit into was my pressure cooker. Of course, I didn't use the lid or there would have been turkey all over the walls.

I got up at five-thirty in the morning to put in on to cook so it would be done by noon. I had to cook it on a wood kitchen range so it was difficult to know how long it would take. It would depend on if the wood would burn and get the fire hot. Well—guess what? It was done by seven-thirty a.m. and almost falling off of the bones. I think "now, what do I do?'—almost five hours until time to serve it. I just stayed up as I had the outside work to do and breakfast to cook. I also had the baby that would soon be awake. I only had one child at the time and I was 20 years old.

My husband had gone rabbit hunting and didn't get home until after four o'clock in the afternoon. I had invited my parents out to

*The canner I cooked the turkey in.*

eat with us along with an aunt. Was I embarrassed when my husband didn't get home until late. We waited until nearly 2 o'clock before we ate without him. My mom helped me finish fixing the meal. So—I learned that a turkey cooks about as fast as a young chicken—fast!!!

# Nurse Maid

When John, my first child was born, I stayed in town at my parents home. He stayed in the hospital for 30 days until he gained weight to weigh five pounds. He was born prematurely. There were no telephones in the country at the time and I needed to be near a telephone if I should be needed by the hospital.

When Jim, my second child was born, we had a lady come in to stay with me for a week after we came home from the hospital, as I had a 14 month old child already at home. You might say that I had my hands full. I had fainted while in the hospital after the birth and they were afraid to leave me alone.

Both Bill and Hattie were working the day shift and couldn't get up at night to help me with the baby. The hired lady as supposed to help me with the baby but I believe she misunderstood. I don't remember John being there. Someone must have taken him for a week.

Old timers believed a new mother was to stay in bed for 10 days and not wash your hair for six weeks. Also I was to wear a girdle for six weeks. I obeyed all the rules with all four of my children and I guess it worked because I still have all the parts I was born with.

Back to the lady—all she ever did was to cook supper. To beat it all—when Bill and Hattie came home from work, they would eat and not offer me a bite until they had eaten. I could hear them in the kitchen talking and laughing. One day they almost forgot to even bring me anything until I mentioned it to her. She never offered me any lunch either. No wonder I lost 14 pounds in two weeks. If I did get up to get a drink of water or some milk, she would grab the glass out of my hand and wash it immediately and turn it upside down on the counter on a dish towel. It kinda made me think she didn't like me using dishes for her to wash. She made biscuits shaped from a little juice glass. Bill and Hattie always bragged on them and she made them everyday. Of course, when I got mine, they were cold.

When it was time to bathe the baby she would bring the water to the bed for me to do it. Ever wash a baby in the bed while trying to balance a pan of water?? Anyway, I thought that was her job, evidently, she didn't think so. At night when the baby cried to be fed, she would wait until I had already gotten up and fixed the bottle, diapered him, and was feeding him when here she would come, all sleepy eyed and saying "I didn't hear the baby." I'd tell her to go back to bed. So much for the extra help with the baby.

She never ran the dust mop or dusted the furniture. I was embarrassed when company come to see the baby. There would be dust balls under the bed. The floors were covered with linoleum and you see the dust on it. That was the last lady we had because I had done most of the care myself, anyway. With the other children, Bill would take a vacation from work and do what was needed to be done to help me. I would wake up from a nap and I would smell kresses that he had gathered and had them on the wood stove cooking. He also washed the clothes both for the children and the baby. You could hear the old washer going and he would be singing. Of course, after 10 days all the extra help was over and I was back to the old grind stone. He was proud of those kids!!

# Old Ways

After my first child was born my mother-in-law insisted that I wear a girdle for six weeks to hold everything in place so I could heal properly. So I obeyed orders and wore one with all four of my children.

I also was not allowed to wash my hair for six weeks. The first two weeks were awful as I could have "clawed" my head until it bled, it would itch so. Then after that it seemed to settle down and you didn't notice it as much. I had long hair that I pulled back in a pony tail so it didn't show how greasy it got. It actually got to feeling good. I really didn't have time to wash it anyway with a new baby, cows to milk, dogs to feed, gardening to do, plus a wood stove to keep fed! And at times cows would not come to the house at milking time and I would have to climb the mountain in search of them.

I had just fed my baby one day and was burping him on my shoulder—when he burped, it seemed like milk came from everywhere—ears, eyes, nose, and mouth. Of course, it only came from his mouth and nose but anyway he was definitely strangled. My mother-in-law happened to walk in about that time and grabbed him by his arm and jerked him up into the air. He immediately coughed and cried and he was all right. I used this method after that if it happened again. I was sure glad she was there. He would have been all right I'm sure but at the time I was scared.

# The Locket

When John was still crawling on the floor as a baby of about seven or eight months old—he would pick up everything and put it in his mouth, as most babies do.

One day he found a heart shaped locket and straight to his mouth it went before I could stop him. I don't know whose it was or where it came from but babies don't miss anything. I was home alone and I didn't know what to do. I tried to keep my "cool" and just stop and think it over. He swallowed it without any problem.

I just picked up the telephone and called my family doctor. He told me to feed him bananas, not just one but several. He told me to watch for it when I changed his diaper as he would pass it in a couple of days. The bananas would make the stool firm and the locket would come out with it.

Sure enough, the next day here came that locket just as the doctor had advised. It didn't look the worse for wear as it came out in the same condition as it was when he swallowed it.

# Neighbor's Dog

We grew a big tobacco patch every year. The patch was across the road in front of our house. We had a neighbor that came up the road in his truck several times a day to check on his cattle and his own tobacco patch. His dog always ran in front of his truck. We would know he was coming before he came around the curve in the road below our house. The dog always ran in the road until it got to our tobacco patch and then it would leave the road and run right through our tobacco, knocking off big leaves as he went.

One day my husband got his rifle and loaded it with buck shot and sat down in a chair to wait for that dog to come. Sure enough, you could hear the truck as it made a lot of noise coming up the road. Just as that dog went to the tobacco patch my husband let loose with that buck shot and it hit it's target. The dog let out a yelp and turned a complete flip. He went on up the road whimpering but that stopped it going in our patch anymore. It would go completely around it to avoid it. The dog wasn't hurt as the buck shot just stings and Bill was a good distance from the dog.

# Killing a Chicken

We always had bantam chickens on our farm. They were more hardy than the large tamer domestic chickens. The bantams could fly for protection from their enemies. They weren't very good for eating for this reason as it made them tough. If I wanted chicken for dinner I had to kill it.

My husband showed me how to clean one and I thought it was interesting and I paid close attention. Little did I know that was my one and only lesson, as the chicken cleaning was turned over to me as was the rabbit and squirrel cleaning.

He never showed me how to kill a chicken, however. I was home alone one day and decided to have chicken for supper. We hadn't had chicken for a while. I got to wanting something besides pork as we usually ate pork from November until April and then mostly vegetables until time to kill hogs again. We had little beef to eat. I was allowed to buy fish at the store but no other meat.

Back to killing this chicken!! I had watched my mom wring a chicken's neck to kill it, but I knew I didn't have the know how for that so I decided to chop it's head off.

The first chore was to catch the blame thing. Ever try to catch a flying chicken by yourself. I finally caught it by hemming it in the coal house. After catching it, I took it to the chopping block and got my ax.

I laid the chicken's head on the chopping block and "sized it up". I had watched Bill and his mother kill them this way. I was perspiring so, I could hardly hold the ax in my hands. I dried my hands on my clothes and proceeded again. My heart was pounding so and I thought I was going to pass out. One of the Ten Commandments, "Thou Shalt Not Kill" kept coming to my mind. Did it mean animals or just humans?? I thought "this is the first thing I have killed that God made." Was I sinning?? Everything ran through my mind telling me not to kill it.

At the same time I needed something for supper. I raised the ax with the chicken looking at me with it's eye showing. Down went the ax and I didn't even look where I was going to hit the chicken. I missed it's neck and got it right across the eye in the middle of it's head. I cut it right into. I quickly hit it again—this time getting it's neck and off came it's head. I turned it loose and it flopped and flopped all over the yard with blood spurting everywhere. I felt as tired as if I had done a day's work. I thought no one should have to go through this to have something to eat.

My family and friends in town got to go to the store and buy their chicken already killed, cleaned, and cut up ready to cook and eat. Of course you've probably guessed, I couldn't eat a bite of it after I cooked it.

I had to heat water on the wood stove to scald it first. What a scent that is!! Next the feathers had to be picked off of it. There were always little fine fluffy feathers that you couldn't pluck out that had to be "singed off". To do this you twisted a paper and caught it on fire with a match and held it and moved the chicken over it to burn off the little fine fuzz.

Next the smelly part as it had to be "gutted" or cleaned. In other words you cut the sucker open and took out it's innards. This was the part that helped to turn me against eating any of it. I just lost my appetite for chicken. Of course, everyone else enjoyed it and ate it all.

I later learned to shoot a rifle. I killed chickens that way from then on. I couldn't handle it with an ax anymore. I got so good with the rifle, I shot a chicken one time in the eye and it came out the other eye on the opposite side of it's head and it dropped over dead.

# Town-confusion

One day my mother-in-law went into town early before she went to work 3-11. She did this on payday sometimes. She started into one of the stores and saw "Tommie" coming out. She said to her "I thought I left you at home." She had mistaken Tommie for me. Was she embarrassed?

# Measuring Windows

There were five large screened windows on our back porch. Every time it rained or snowed it would blow in on the floor and make a mess. I decided it needed to be enclosed with glass windows. I got out my handy little ruler and measured the screened space. They were each one a different size. I took my measurements to town and ordered windows to fit those spaces.

They cost me the grand amount of $4.00 each—that is with the glass and the wooden frame. I took them home and put them in place. Do you know they every one fit?? All I had to do was secure them so they wouldn't fall out. I put a nail in four places to keep them in place. They worked perfect for several years. My husband never one time mentioned them to me and I don't even know if he noticed them. They helped relieve me a lot of work and the porch was warmer.

# Feeding Pigs

I used to hate to feed the pigs. I guess it was the chore I liked the least. The pigs would always jump up on the side of the pen and squeal. They would sling whatever was on their feet all over you.

One Saturday I had taken a bath and washed my hair and was going to take the afternoon off from work. I had put on a pair of sexy red, white, and blue striped pants. I had forgot that the pigs had to be fed. Well—here I go to the pen and sure enough they come on the side of the pen and threw "brown muck" all over my clean pants. Was I ever upset!!!

# Pouting

My husband used to be the easiest person to pout. One morning when he got up I was feeding the baby his breakfast. He was in the high chair and I had just put the egg yolk into the baby cereal. I was beginning to feed him and wanted to finish before it got cold. We only had a wood stove that I had boiled the egg on and I had no way to reheat it. No electric stove or microwave. My husband asked for his breakfast and I answered, "can you wait a few minutes until I finish this?" Well—no answer.

He went back to the bedroom and then came back to the kitchen in his outside work clothes that consisted of a pair of overalls, long sleeve shirt and boots. He walked through the kitchen and out to the garden by the barn. After I finished feeding the baby I put him down with a bottle. I prepared my husband's breakfast and went to the garden and told him that it was ready. No answer!!! I went back into the house and started lunch, as I stated before, I had to pack a lunch from the table. And Bill was working 3-11. I kept his breakfast warm in the warmer on top of the stove. He never did come in for his breakfast or even mention it again.

He came in for lunch and ate without speaking a single word. He changed his clothes and went to work without saying "good-bye" or anything. It kind of upset me but then I thought "how silly!" Believe it or not he refused breakfast the rest of the week. This was the entire time he worked 3-11 which was five days. He finally broke down and acted normal again.

He was not a person to apologize. I guess his "male ego" was touched. He would pout also if you ever raised your voice to him. He could be difficult at times. I just learned to live with it. But were those overalls sexy!!! Today couples refer to this as "getting the silent treatment."

# New Calf

I was the record keeper of our animals birthing due date. This was mostly because I was always home and knew when they were bred. I would mark it on the calendar and when it came nearly time for the birth I would keep an eye on them to be prepared for trouble with their birthing. I was pretty accurate as I didn't miss many times.

One such time one of our young cows had a calf in the dead of winter. She had it down across the creek in the rhododendron thicket where it was away from the wind. I had to go through a three acre field and across the creek to get to them. The calf was born about three o'clock in the afternoon.

About five o'clock I became concerned because I could see it trying to walk and it kept falling down. I was afraid it would stumble and fall in the creek and not be able to get out and maybe freeze to death or drown. A calf is very unsteady on it's feet for a while after it is born. It was wobbling around and falling down so I went to get it.

I bodily carried that calf to the barn that was located close to the house. I would have to stop and let it down on the ground every little bit as it was heavy. The wind was cold and snow was blowing in my face. I finally got it to the barn with the mother cow following me and bawling all the time. I knew I'd be to blame if something happened to it. I had no other choice. The children were not old enough or big enough to be of any help. The dumb mother cow didn't offer to move it anywhere else away from the creek.

Well—a couple of days later—I got bronchitis with a head cold. I kept it about two weeks. Then one day my chest on the left began to feel sore. It progressed until it hurt to breathe or raise my arm. It progressed finally to the point to where I couldn't even lift my arm to put away dishes on a shelf.

I went to the doctor and he said I had side pleurisy. I had to go to his office to lay under a heat lamp and take heat treatments every other day for over a month. I had to wear a rib belt or binder all the time day and night. I couldn't milk the cow or do anything much.

Bill took over the chores including the cooking. He didn't believe in buying groceries from the store. He always cooked from the can house. It consisted of canned green beans, stewed potatoes and corn bread. He cooked them on the wood cook stove. I usually poured part of the juice the beans were canned in off but he always cooked the beans with all the juice. Canned beans are good but the juice sometimes can be offensive to the smell. When I would open the door when I came home from the doctor and he was cooking, the smell of those green beans hit me. They had an odor all their own.

After several days of this I thought I would gag if I smelled another green bean cooking. It really burned me out and today I am not really fond of canned green beans. Those days are gone forever. He was really trying to be helpful and it did help—but man—I'd have loved to have had some meat or something different every once in a while. I was glad when I recovered from that ailment. If the ailment or treatment didn't kill me—the food would. I should be thankful—but after all too much of a good thing isn't good anymore.

# Pink Eye

As I seemed to be in charge of taking care of the farm animals, one day I noticed one of our new calves with the pink eye. The eyes water and it runs down their face leaving it looking nasty. It will blind them if it goes untreated. The white of the eye turns deep pink. To treat this we usually just throw table salt in them.

To catch the crazy animal was another thing. I sometimes could just walk up to it and throw the salt at it and it usually "hit its mark".

Treating a calf is a little different as a calf is very jumpy. I chased the calf through the woods along a "cow trail" hoping to treat it. No such luck. It had other ideas. So I walked behind it slowly and quickly just bodily grabbed it by the ears and made it stop. I went a few steps before completely stopping. I was hanging on for dear life. I was able to get my hand in my pocket into my bag of salt and get some into its eyes. I turned him loose and away it went. Can you believe this from this little town girl?

# Ramp Hunting

Bill would take me and the children on little trips close to home. We would walk on these trips as they were usually to the woods.

One spring he decided to take us ramp hunting. I was ready to go just about anywhere as I had to stay home so much. We started out one morning at dawn. We got up early and did the milking and feeding the pigs. I was to take a cake of fresh baked corn bread. We were going to eat this for our lunch along with the ramps we were going to find.

Starting out we climbed straight up the mountain behind our house. It seemed like it went up to the sky, it was so steep. From there it leveled off but it was a constant climb over rocks (some very big) and through the bushes and through the woods for it seemed like forever through the woods. I was glad it was early in the spring and snakes weren't out yet. I would have been miserable keeping an eye out for them. Remember I had four children with me. He did show us a fox den along the way.

It took us until lunch time to get to where the ramps were. They were very easy to pull out. We just pulled the outer skin off and ate them with our cornbread. We found a little spring of water that we drank with it. We were hungry so it tasted pretty good! It was close to 4 p.m. when we got home. We had walked the whole time. Some trip!! I only did this once as once was enough. We had to take turns carrying one of the younger children as they tired easier than the older ones.

# The Scours

A baby calf sometimes get the "scours", a term used for diarrhea that if not corrected could kill the calf. This happens if the cows milk is too rich for the calf to tolerate. To stop this we would put a cup of flour into a frying pan and let it scorch until it turned lightly brown in color. We then let it cool and fed it to the calf with a spoon. You have to hold it down to get it in them. It usually takes two people. This treatment worked every time for us.

# Vacation

Every year during the Fourth of July, my brother who lived in Texas, brought his family home to North Carolina on vacation. He had four daughters at the time. His son hadn't been born when this incident happened. Two of the girls usually came to stay with me. One went with my sister and the other girl went to stay with our sister-in-law. My brother and his wife, Jeannie, stayed with our parents in town. The same two girls came to stay with us each year.

They liked it in the country. They went swimming in the creek, rode bicycles, and just generally played. One day we were on the front porch and a cow we had was expecting a calf and we could see her over on the hill from the house. When she finally had the calf, my niece Carolyn, yelled "look, that cow just laid a calf." Of course, we laughed and teased her and said, "silly, cows don't lay calves, they just have them." She was a town girl and knew nothing of the words used to describe the birth of cattle.

As kids will, they followed Bill when he went to the garden. One day he put them to work. He told them to get the cabbage worms out of the cabbages and kill them by pulling them apart or mashing them. They were usually big, fat, and green from eating the cabbage.

Carolyn likes to tell the tale about the cabbage worms. She said she went to the table at lunch very hungry. She knew I was making a fresh blackberry pie and her mouth was watering. The sad part was that I wouldn't let her have pie until she ate her lunch of which it just happened to be cooked cabbage. She said every time she would get that cabbage to her mouth she would think of those big fat green worms and she couldn't eat it. She got her pie as I had no intention of depriving her of it. You see I didn't know that she had killed cabbage worms all morning. I was in the house and just knew they were with Bill. I didn't know what they were doing.

# Tobacco

Bill started raising tobacco a few years after we got married. Everyone who lived near us did. His mother had an allotment so we used hers. If you don't raise any tobacco for three years, they could take away the allotment and give it to someone else. No tobacco had been raised for two years so to save hers, we decided to give it a try. We had to pay her so much of the money that we made off of it for payment for using her allotment. I believe we paid her 1/3. We would make about 6 - 700 dollars off of .3 acre. Her part would be about 200 dollars.

In early spring, about February or March, a tobacco bed had to be made ready to grow the plants. You cleared the ground and put a wooden frame around it. Over this frame you attached a plastic cover. You then spray under this to kill weeds and other undesirables. You let this stay for several days. Then you remove the plastic and plant the little tobacco seeds. You then cover it back up with a cheese cloth and leave it until the plants grow and are nearly ready to transplant.

It is usually the middle of May to the first of June before they are ready. The are then moved to the tobacco field. Each plant has to be watered when it is set out and the dirt pressed securely around it to cover the roots.

We planted our whole patch one day in the rain. It was a soft warm rain and this relieved us from having to carry water from the branch for them. It took us all day. Bill and I planted until noon. He was working the graveyard shift and didn't go to bed. We just started setting out plants after the children caught the school bus. When they came home at 4 o'clock, Bill got back up and wanted to set more plants. He said he couldn't sleep any longer knowing what a nice rain we were having and he had to plant some more tobacco. We worked in the field until after dark that day. Guess what?? We planted the whole patch before we quit. And every one lived but about two. We only tried that once as it had to be hard on him to work all night after about four hours of sleep. If we had extra plants we shared with our neighbors and they would do the same.

On one particular day I was helping Bill with the tobacco bed and our cat was there with us. He caught a little ground squirrel but he didn't kill it. He just played with it. He would turn it loose and then when it would start to run off the cat would catch it again. He did this several times and I kept dreading for him to catch it as I just knew he was going to kill it right before my eyes. He let it go one time too many, however, because that squirrel saw his chance and made a "high-dive" for the first bush and got away. Was that cat ever surprised!! Frankly, I was glad as I felt sorry for that squirrel being teased that way.

The tobacco would grow all summer until about July, then it would have to be suckered. To do this you break out all the new stems and leaves trying to grow and then we "topped" it by breaking off the top of the plant. This would let the tobacco leaves that were left to grow bigger and spread out.

We then cut the tobacco, stalks and all. It was taken by truck to the barn and hung on the rafters to stay there to dry out and cure. About the last of October it would be ready to class and take to the market to sell. We had to grade it on damp mornings or on a rainy day. Dampness made it come in "case" or soft enough to handle without falling apart.

The first year that we grew the tobacco, we stored it in a spare bedroom. The house had been divided into two sections and two families had lived in it. There was a porch and a door leading from each side of the house. The empty side was where we stored the tobacco. We also graded it there too. Our first crop was a small one as we were just learning. It would take the better part of the year just growing this tobacco. After we started using the barn to store the tobacco, if any tobacco fell and we didn't see it, the dogs would make a bed on it.

The money helped pay our taxes and buy Christmas gifts. I spent many a day in the tobacco field suckering and topping tobacco. I wore a rain coat to keep my clothes dry as I would start early in the morning after the school bus ran. My hair would be sticky with the tobacco juice and my hands would nearly stick together with it. As the morning progressed, it would get terribly hot. Then I would be wet with perspiration. Man, I hated that job!!

# Home Brew

As I stated before, my husband loved to play jokes on people. I also mentioned the boys he hung out with. To explain this— these boys all grew up in the country. They all went to the same grammar school and rode the school bus home together. When World War II started, they all joined either the Navy, Army, or the Marines. They played cow pasture football and softball in a local pasture. So as adults, they still kinda hung together. Especially since one of them opened a grocery and gas store after he came home from the service. This is where they hung out. They had a place to pitch horse shoes in good weather. They played some penny poker at night and probably shared a bottle and some wild stories.

One year Bill decided to make some home brew. It was supposed to be a substitute for beer. Someone in the mill had told him how to make it. He was one to try anything once. He was like that. That is another reason I couldn't leave my kraut in the crock.

It was always needed for something. Old timers didn't can their kraut or pickle beans. They just ate it from the crock.

Well, back to the home brew. It was made with something he bought in town. It was a can that held about 16 oz. He used about four of them. It had no taste. It looked like molasses but it wasn't. It was called "malt" I think. He put it in the 5 gallon crock with water and a pack of yeast. It was covered with a clean white cloth and put in the dark to ferment or "work" for about ten days to two weeks.

One day I looked out and there stood about five of Bill's friends on our back porch. He asked for some glasses. They had come to sample the home brew. It was about ready. They each drank about two glasses. They smacked their lips and bragged on how good it was. No one noticed that Bill wasn't drinking any. He only tasted it. After they left, Bill laughed and said, "They'll think good when they get the bellyache tonight." Only one came back for seconds and he came every day until it was gone.

Bill sometimes made grape wine if there were any grapes left when I got through making grape juice and jelly. He couldn't stand to see anything go to waste on the vine—be it beans, potatoes, or grapes. I made 10 gallons of grape juice one year. That's 20 ½ gallon jars full. It come in handy in the winter when there is snow on the ground and a big bowl of popped corn.

By the way, I even grew popcorn one year. It had to dry on the cob before we could pop it. Back to the wine—he would wash the grapes after they were taken off the stems. He had the children crushing them before putting them in the crock. He'd add water enough to cover only—add a pack of yeast and about 2 ½ pounds of sugar. It was covered and set in a cool place to ferment.

Talk about smelling good. If you drank it too soon before it was through working, it would give you diarrhea. You could tell if you sampled it and it effected you that way, then it wasn't ready to drink. It was a good tonic. It helped your appetite, any elimination problems and about ½ of a juice glass at bedtime helped you to sleep. Some folks would say that homemade wine is an alcoholic beverage because of the yeast. Don't ask me—it's just something I heard. It would make you more depressed and easy to cry.

# Car

One of my best friends in high school had a car she got to drive. Her dad had a company car as he was a wood buyer for Champion. His job was to scout out wood for the company to buy to use in their mill. So they provided him the car as he had to be on the road so much. This left the family car at home for my friend and her mother to drive. It was a Pontiac.

This was during a time when girls didn't smoke in public. Since my friend liked to smoke and I didn't, she would let me drive the car. She would stop in front of the high school outside the city limits. Of course, school would be out—as it was after school. She would let me behind the wheel and she would sit in the passenger side.

Now this car wasn't an automatic. I had to change gears and learn to master the clutch. It didn't take me long to learn it but we got jarred up a little bit while I was learning. She taught me how to let the clutch out and press on the gas and off we would go. When we got near home she would take the wheel again.

We would drive to Bethel on the river road and back to town on the main road. I guess that's how I survived not learning to smoke. I had rather drive than smoke. We charged the gas to her dad's account. When it got too high we had to start pitching in and help to pay for it. We did a lot of joy riding and her parents thought it wasn't necessary. You know how teenagers are though. We were no different.

One day I was sailing along up the river road and approached this hill. As we came over it here came a car right at us. I threw on the brakes and stopped on a dime to avoid hitting it. We both agree after that to keep our foot always near the brake to avoid further mishaps.

After I married I used to practice on the dirt road that ran by our house. I would go up the road to turn around. I would back into a creek and go back home and park the car and no one knew I had moved it. My husband would be in the bed sleeping after working graveyard the night before. What my friend showed me to do helped me to teach myself to drive.

One day I asked Bill if I could go and try for my license. He was surprised and said "you can't drive." I said, "Well, I can too." O.K.

he said, "show me." So I got behind the wheel and my husband, with a friend of his, got in the car and off we go. I did so well he told me to drive to town. I did with no problem. The next day he took me to try for my driver's license and I passed. Was he surprised!! I have never had a wreck so my self teaching must not have been too bad. Most of the credit I have to give to my friend for letting me drive her car and showing me how.

# Leather Britches

I always had plenty of green beans in the summer from our garden. After I canned all I thought I needed in jars or I would run out of jars I would find other ways to preserve the ones left. I made pickle beans with some and then I would dry some to make "Shucky beans" or "Leather Britches".

To make these I would string the clean, washed, dry beans on a thread strong enough to hold them. It would be about a foot and one half long. They were then hung out to dry. On sunny days I put them in the sun to help them dry quicker. If they dried slow they could spoil and mold. After they dried we stored them in a clean sack in the can house. When I wanted to cook them, I would soak them overnight as you do dried beans today. They are cooked as dried beans are today also, with a piece of "fat back" and salt to taste.

# Pickled Beans

To make pickle beans you break and blanch them just as you would if you were going to can them. The difference is, you pour the water off of them and let them get completely cold. If you don't they will sour. The beans have to be cooked about ½ done, but still slightly crisp. You cover them with cool water and put canning salt on top. These beans are put in a crock for about a week to two weeks to get sour. You can heat and can them then, or just leave in the crock until all eaten. To eat them you heat them with oil or bacon grease for seasoning. Delicious with cornbread and potatoes. They come in handy on a snowy day when you can't get to town.

# Tobacco Bed-garden

One spring I happened to mention as to why we had to have a garden every year. I was just plain tired of canning all summer every year and very few of my friends in town had to make a garden. They got to go to the swimming pool in town and I never did. The reply was "if there's no garden you can just do without this winter." I didn't say anymore about it. As Bill's father had died young it made it hard on them and I guess they depended on the garden to help them survive the winter.

We made the tobacco bed and when the plants were ready, we planted them as usual. We usually planted the garden about the same time. No mention was made of it, however. I began to think about it and it worried me. The garden wasn't plowed and I couldn't do it.

I decided to plant some cabbage and peas in the tobacco bed. The soil was soft and ready and needed little preparation. The cabbage grew so I decided to try some beans. They came up hardy so I added corn, squash, and cucumbers. I got four "Big Boy" tomato plants and put them near the four fence posts around the tobacco bed. They grew so tall they were taller than the posts. I guess there were at least five bushels of tomatoes harvested from those vines. Not a spot on them.

Bill took an interest after I got things growing. I planted "McAslan Pole" beans so they would grow near the fence. My plan was for them to climb the fence. It turned out that the plan was a good one, as I could pick beans from both sides of the fence. When I wanted a mess of those beans all I had to do was cross the road, go through the fence to the tobacco patch and go to the tobacco bed and pick a mess of beans. These beans grew about 1 to 1 ½ feet long. I would pick them and carry them home like an arm load of wood. I didn't need a basket for them. I could break them and have them on to cook in just a few minutes. They didn't have strings on them, so all I had to do was break them up. They would cook in just about an hour.

I made a very good little garden in just a small space, so it can be done. I never complained again about the garden. I figured it was just meant to be and I learned to live with it. I believe a higher power intervened and made everything grow so good that year.

# Polk Salad

L iving in the country you have certain foods you gather at certain
times of the year. Some are kresses and polk salad. Kresses are
gathered from corn fields usually in early spring before gardens are
plowed. Polk salad is gathered after gardens are planted but before
cabbage or anything is ready to eat from the garden. After a winter
without many fresh greens or green vegetables, we looked forward
to getting to pick them. People would come from town to go to the
corn field and get them with permission of the owners, of course.

One day I decided to cook polk salad for supper. No one was home
but me. The children were at school and their dad was at work. I had
noticed my neighbors had also gone to town. So—I go out looking
for my supper. I was breaking off stalks of polk and filling my bag.
Well—I looked up on the bank and it was covered with polk. Some
of the prettiest I had ever seen. I had to have it.

I was picking away then I got this feeling that I wasn't alone. Have
you ever had that feeling? I would stop and look around but didn't
see anything. I picked some more, getting most of what was in reach.
I still felt like someone was watching me. I would look at my
neighbor's porch where they usually sat but as I said they had gone
to town. I looked up the road and all around me but didn't see
anyone. I had to start jumping up to get to the polk because it was
getting out of my reach. I got several nice pieces and started to reach
for some more, by climbing on the bank. I reached for the polk to
be stopped in mid-air by two black beady eyes looking straight at me.
The biggest black snake was laying there right where my hand was
going. I froze momentarily looking directly into that snake's eyes. I
still see them today. It was laying spread out up the side of the bank.
I jumped down from that bank, threw the bag half full of polk down
and literally skimmed over the creek getting out of there. Forget the
polk for supper. I've never gathered polk again to this day.

# Peeper

One day I was lying in the sun trying to get a suntan while the children were taking a nap. I kept hearing a chicken "peeping", so—I sat up and tried to determine where it was coming from. It seemed to be coming from the pasture above the house. So I got up to search for it. I found it by following the direction of the sound of "peeping". It was in a deserted hen nest.

It had apparently hatched late after the other eggs and the mother hen had taken the others and left the nest. She was no where to be seen. So I took the little yellow chicken home to tend to it. Leaving it there, it didn't have a chance. At night I would put it in a box in the kitchen with a paper over it. I would also put a warm bottle or water in a jar with a lid on it in the box. The chicken would snuggle up to it to keep warm and for comfort. Every three hours the water would get cold and it would start crying loudly. I would have to get up to reheat the water and then quietness would prevail until it got cold again.

Tending to a baby chicken is almost like getting up to feed a new baby. This chicken was so spoiled it wouldn't even defend itself. We had dogs and cats so I couldn't turn it out in the yard. They would attack it as would the other chickens. It lived in an open box on the porch during the day. As it grew it learned how to protect itself better. I guess it being bigger in size also didn't attract anything to bother it.

It learned to crow. It would get outside our bedroom window at daylight and crow until you got up and went outside and attempted to run it off. It would come right back, and it got plenty of practice a crowing right under that window. We put up with it for several months in the summer.

When fall was approaching my husband decided to give him to a friend that lived down the road. Later we asked about the chicken or rooster as it turned out to be. The man said the rooster woke up at 4 o'clock every morning right outside the bedroom window. Then one day when they couldn't take it any longer, he was put in the pot and chicken and dumplings were made out of him. Poor little Peeper. That was the name I gave him.

# Potatoes

We always had a big potato patch. It would yield about 20 bushels of potatoes and they were good sized potatoes. We would dig them in the fall and store them in burlap sacks (Toe Sack). We would stack them on top of each other and the rest we would put in bushel baskets and store them in our can house. We ate them all by Spring and they never went to waste.

I also gathered apples in bushel baskets and pears from a neighbor's tree. If you have never made a pear cobbler, you're missing something. You make it like any other cobbler except you put lemon juice in it and it makes the taste out of this world.

A friend of my husband's wasn't very thrifty with his money and he never made a garden so before payday he usually ran out of food. He would come to our potato patch after we gathered all we could find. He would go through the ground again and find more potatoes we had missed. All they ever ate came from a store as they never put anything up for a rainy day.

We tried growing sweet potatoes but you need loose soil for them and they never did any good for us. Bill would bring home a bushel from the Farmer's Market and spread them in our attic to cure. Talk about sweet and good after about six weeks. They tasted like they had been injected with sugar. I forgot to mention that they were white sweet potatoes.

# Washing Machine

Outside of the city limits you have to use well water. Water pipes to city homes providing them water do not extend to the country. That makes it difficult to have an automatic washing machine. Water is pumped from the well with an electric pump and if you run the water too long you get the pump waterlogged. This means the pump won't shut off and it could catch on fire and burn up. If the pump gets waterlogged a repair man has to be called to fix it.

My husband watched them a time or two, then he learned how to repair it himself. It was an old pump and this happened quite frequently. It was also impossible to take a shower. When my mother-in-law moved out and went to town to live she left her old washer with us. It was about worn out anyway. The lid was rusty and the kids used it to sleigh ride on.

When the washer gave out my husband went to town to get another one. I dared not hope for an automatic washer, but I hoped anyway. I visualized a pretty new automatic washer. I knew the well probably couldn't carry it but I wished for a miracle. All of my friends had an automatic washer but me. Well—here he comes around the curve and up the road home from town with the washer. There sitting proudly in the back of the truck was a brand new wringer washer. I could have cried. I knew it would be years now before I got an automatic washing machine.

# Wine

There was a man in our community that raised tobacco but he didn't have a way to get it to market. Bill, my husband, would take it for him. He never took payment for it. One day he took him and on the way home he wanted to stop and get a bottle of whiskey. He offered to get Bill some and he refused it. So here he comes out of the ABC store with a bottle of strawberry wine. He said "give this to Jody."

Well that night Bill went out with his buddies. It used to bother me when he did this as I had to stay home all the time with the kids. After he left and I got the kids to bed, I decided to try the wine. Mind you, I had never drank any before. I poured the first glass and drank it immediately as I was thirsty. It really tasted good. Well—one glass led to another. I was sitting in a chair watching TV. It tasted like strawberry soda.

*A bottle of wine.*

I had nearly drunk the whole bottle when I decided to get up and go to the bathroom. I attempted to get up only to find I was very dizzy and unsteady on my feet. I had to crawl to the bathroom. When I got there I not only had to go to the bathroom but I proceeded to throw up. I guess I threw up the whole bottle of wine I had drunk. About that time Bill came home. He looked at the bottle and couldn't believe I had drunk the whole thing. You know I wasn't even sick the next day. I guess it all came back so fast it didn't have time to make me sick.

# Snake In The Road

One Sunday afternoon Bill was at work and the children were playing. I was sitting in the front porch swing. I noticed something moving through the field that ran below the road. There was a creek of water that paralleled it. I watched the movement only to see that it was a snake, or so it seemed. It was moving ever so slow. It took about ten minutes for it to cross the field. It crawled on up to the road and I had to stand up to see for I couldn't believe my eyes. The biggest, fattest black snake I had ever seen was there. It took another ten minutes for it to cross the road. At one point in time it spanned the entire road from side to side. I thought, "boy, if a car

*I was sitting on the porch in the swing. The snake came through the field from the creek at the left of the picture and crossed the road at the center of the picture. It went up the hill in the far right of the picture. Cindy is sitting on the steps.*

comes around the curve, you're a goner." No car came, however and it continued to crawl up the bank into the pasture above the road. It was also very big around. It took at least thirty minutes for this snake to disappear. I was scared at first then I saw how slow it was moving and I knew it would never catch me.

When my husband and mother-in-law came in from work I told them about it. I was so afraid they would not believe me. Instead they said, "yes, there is a big black snake that's been here for years. It doesn't bother anything." It just ate field mice and water and field snakes. It probably did—because I never did see a poisonous snake the whole nineteen years I lived out there. My son has seen a black snake in the field where he lives out there today. Probably an offspring from it.

# Old Barn

On a hill across from our house was an old barn that a family lived in. It had a dirt floor and no water in the house or any bath facilities. They washed their clothes in the creek. They were tenement farmers raising tobacco. They later moved into a tenant house when one came available that was on up the road a good ways from our house. The children turned out all right after starting from such a humble beginning.

# Cat - Ditto

We had a cat we called Ditto. He was part Maltese and was a beautiful gray without any other marking. He was solid gray. My daughter had wanted a cat so her dad brought her one home one afternoon. It was just a little kitten. We had to keep it in the house until it got big enough to protect itself.

One night the beagle dogs woke me up barking. I got up and looked out the window. The moon was full and you could see outside as it was as clear as if it had been daylight. I looked and looked trying to see why the dogs were barking. I finally saw Ditto across the creek and on the hill, walking slowly. So that's what the dogs were taking on so over.

I opened the door and yelled out real loud, Ditto!!! He stopped and looked my way and then proceeded on his way. He would stay out all night and then come to the living room window to be let into the house. He would sleep all day. You could vacuum all around him and he wouldn't even wake up. I even picked him up and moved him to another pillow on another chair and he wouldn't wake up until he was good and ready.

# Worst Nightmare

One summer morning we awoke to a damp foggy morning. As the fog begin to rise, we could see the garden over on the hill. I was horrified to see the horse and about six cows standing in the garden. They had stripped the corn from the stalks and stomped the rest of the garden. Our corn was just coming in too. We had just had our first mess of good fresh corn. I had canned a lot of beans already and the tomatoes were at the bottom of the garden and they didn't bother them much.

What happened—Bill had been working 3-11 and hadn't had time to check the fence around the garden. He admitted later that he knew one of the stakes was loose as he had noticed the horse leaning over it once before. He had just neglected to fix it. Nevertheless— me and the kids got blamed for it. He wouldn't speak to any of us for over a week. The kids were small and I sure couldn't fix a fence. I felt we were blamed wrongly but what's passed is passed.

# Another Nightmare

In the winter we usually put our cows in the barn out of the weather. This particular incident happened because we had tobacco curing in one of the stalls. My son had tied our milk cow on the outside of one of the stalls. It was slightly sloped where the cow stood. During the night evidently the cow had slipped and fell down and couldn't get back on her feet.

*The smoke house behind the children where I saw the two black snakes. It was just a short way from the house as the back door to the house is to the left of the picture. This is a picture of a late snow with my children playing in it.*

When my son went out to milk her the next morning he found her strangled to death. She was in a position as if she had struggled to get her footing back. She had dug a gully in the ground where her feet kept slipping. Of course, we got blamed for this too. These were young boys doing a man's job. Yes, you're right. We got the silent treatment again.

# More Snakes

We had a smoke house that stood right outside our kitchen door. We kept our "streaked" meat that we covered in salt to preserve it and our hams that were curing hung from the ceiling.

One day I went out to the shed to get a piece of meat to cook with green beans for supper. I started to open the door when I happened to look down and see something black sticking out from under the corner of the building. I saw it was a snake. Of course—I got scared as I was home alone. The children were at school and Bill was at work.

I really needed the meat to cook supper—so I called my neighbor to come and help me. He and his wife came to the house carrying a hoe. He told her to open the door and get out of the way. I was standing back watching. She opened the door and he hit at the snake with the hoe and "addled it". Were we ever surprised when we discovered that there were two instead of one. They were wound around each other making it difficult for them to get away. He killed them both. One of them had a frog in its mouth with one of its legs eaten off. We got the frog out of the snakes mouth but it was already dead. What a terrible way to die!!!

*The arrow points to the tree that had the tire swing.*

# Tire Swing

There was a tall oak tree in the pasture, across the creek, and high on the hill. In this tree, Bill hung a long rope and then tied it to an old automobile tire. Our children would swing on it and it would go over the land below. It would swing so slow and easy. The tree still stands today.

# Young Bull

We kept between ten and twelve cows at a time. When their calves got about six weeks old we would sell them for veal. We kept a bull calf one time until he was over a year old. He got so big and lazy and he would lay around in the pasture in the sun. The children could feed him salt from their hands and they would climb on his back when he was lying down. He never moved. They would rub his ears and sometimes they would be two at a time on him. He never offered once to hurt them. He was just a big pet.

# Trick or Treat

I always took my children Trick or Treating on Halloween. I made them a costume and off we would go. Right before it got dark we

*The children were coming down the road to the right. The hole he went into is on the left of the road. I was sitting in a car down the road to the left of the hole.*

would get in the car and start out. I learned, after a few Halloweens, to make a costume that was warm. It would be warm right up until the night before and then it would turn off cold, and would usually mist some rain. I would take them to an area and wait in the car for them.

One particular night, I was watching for them to return to the car. Here they came—down the road—running and excited about their treat. I could see shadows because it was dark by then. I saw a shadow of all four of them when all of a sudden one of them disappeared from sight, just like he had fell into a hole. Well—only three children came to the car. They were all there but one. In a few minutes here he came. He was crawling out of a ditch he had ran into—feet first. He wasn't hurt and neither were his treats. He still had his bag in his hand. It was funny to see someone running and then literally sink out of sight. Luckily, he wasn't hurt. He was young and a survivor.

# Hog Killing

We always got two small baby pigs in the spring of the year to fatten up to be killed in the fall for our winter meat. We killed them the first real cold day of winter. For years we killed them ourselves, always on a Saturday. Four or five of Bill's friends or neighbors would get them a bottle of whiskey, supposedly to keep them warm as they worked outside in the cold.

They would get a big barrel and put it close to the branch and would fill it with water and build a fire under it. It had to be a certain temperature or it would "set" the hair on the pigs. When the water got hot enough they would shoot the pigs and then put them in the hot water to loosen the hair on their backs. The hair was removed and the pigs were hung up on a pole and the abdomen cut open. The abdomen contents were removed. The liver was washed and then brought to me to fry some fresh liver for lunch. The rest of the insides were thrown away.

The liver was a big thing—as big as a gallon bucket. I would slice enough for lunch and wash it again before I fried it coated in cornmeal. It was really good. The rest of the fresh liver was hung up on a nail until I got time to make the rest up in liver mush. Liver doesn't keep very long and has to be cooked to help preserve it. I didn't have a freezer so I had to cook it.

I had to can the sausage and the ribs. The meat was cut up in pieces and took to town to be made into sausage and seasoned with sage and salt. Sausage was made from scrapes of meat and a big ham being ground up. There would be two large pans of it. I would fry it almost done and then pack it in jars, put the lid on and then turn the jar upside down to cool. This made the grease come to the top of the jar and maked a better seal so it wouldn't spoil. The hams and shoulders were salted and cured with brown sugar and hung to cure for weeks. The bacon and fat back were salted for use in beans and to cook for breakfast in the winter.

It was usually a three day process with me working at it all day and into the night. I was using a wood cook stove. I had to cook all the white pieces of fat to make lard. This lard made the best biscuits and cakes you ever ate. They were so light they could float. We ate pork until spring of the year or until it ran out.

I gave the head to my mom to make souse meat. I didn't like souse meat and I wouldn't eat it. It was made from the head and tongue and the thought didn't appeal to me. She would cook the head and then take the meat off of it and grind it and cook it with cornmeal and make a big pan of souse meat.

I pickled the feet for my husband but he wouldn't eat them unless he was about "2 shades in the wind". That's a term for drinking. I hated pigs feet because all I could see was those pigs standing knee deep in their own filth.

Good pork chops and tenderloin were my fa-

*Would you like to ride a pig backwards that is this big??*

vorite. When the hams were cured we ate ham at least every day for breakfast or lunch. It was delicious. Those were the days. A good education but I don't want to repeat it.

After we discovered we could get the pigs killed in a meat packing house in Asheville, we started taking them there. It was a lot less work for me. The trick was to get the pigs loaded and taken over there.

One morning after working graveyard, my husband came home to load the pigs. He brought a friend with him to help. Well—he decided to turn the pigs loose in the field and drive them into the back of the truck. What possessed him to do this I'll never know to this day. A pig is not that easy to drive as they soon found out. The pig ran around the field for a while and then decided to come up into the road. I was standing there watching.

It started running toward me and I knew if it got by me it would run away off down the road and may never get caught. So I got a big stick and proceeded to try to stop it. Well—that pig had a mind of it's own and didn't intend to be caught. It ran right at me and I swung that stick and it just broke like a toothpick. On came the pig—right at me. I couldn't believe my eyes—the closer it got to me. That pig ran right between my legs and lifted me up in the air onto it's back. It didn't even slow down—if anything it got faster. I guess I rode that dumb pig backwards at least two car lengths before I finally fell off. The road was gravel and all that saved me was the soft shoulder of the road with grass on it. I landed right next to a barbed wire fence. I only skinned my hands where I tried to cushion my fall. Talk about an angel on my shoulder—I had to have had one—just about the whole time I lived in the country. I wasn't hurt but my pride was.

We finally hemmed the pig in the barn and got it loaded. At least I stopped it from going down the road to who knows where. That was the last time any pigs were turned loose to be loaded. He backed the truck up to the pen like he should have the first time. We let the meat processing plant pack the meat to be frozen, thus ending my having to can it.

Of course, we didn't have a freezer and we had to rent a freezer locker to store it. Instead of going to the store when I needed meat, I just went to the locker. Talk about being cold in there!! You had to wear a coat when you went inside for meat or else you could only stay for a few short minutes. You would have to come outside in the sun and warm up and go back in. It was a big freezer locker room.

# Milk

We always kept a cow so we could have our own milk. It was rare if we didn't have a cow to milk year round. A week after I moved to the country that was my job after I learned how. At one time I had three cows to milk. It was morning and night—twice a day. The two older boys helped me before they caught the school bus in the morning. We had a light cord that reached the barn to have light to see by as it was dark in the winter at six in the morning. Only one of the cows was a good one. The other two would kick and misbehave.

When a cow is "fresh" she will give 1 ½ gallons at a milking. We would milk her until about a month before she was due to "come in" or give birth again. We just let her "dry up" as she was giving just a small amount of milk anyway. She would be giving barely enough for us to use. We would buy milk for about a month until she "came in" or had her calf. When we milked three cows my refrigerator would be full with at least ten gallons of milk at a time. I had to take the two bottom shelves out of the refrigerator to make room for it. I kept it in ½ gallon jars with lids.

I sold milk to two of Bill's aunts and their husbands. I also sold to my older brother that lived just down the road from me. When his wife would come for the milk she would "snitch" a couple of my tomatoes that I would have ripening in the window on the back porch. She would just politely pick them up as she went out the door. He also would ask to buy blackberries from me. He seemed to think they were good for your stomach. He had a history of ulcers. One of Bill's aunts got milk every day while the other one only got it about three times a week. I got 25 cents a half gallon.

*An old churn*

After one day the cream would "rise" to the top of the jar and what was on the bottom was called "blue john". That would be the same as skim milk today. I would pour the cream off the top of the day old milk and put it in a crock jar to sour and thicken to churn in a couple of days. The time of the year determined how often I would have to churn. In the summer it would get ready quicker. This was called "clabbered milk". Then it was ready to churn. One of Bill's aunts would not let me get through churning before they would be there wanting fresh buttermilk and butter.

In the summer I had to think up a different way to churn as I had other chores to do that were just as important. There was always something to can in the summer. The pigs, dog, and cat got the milk I didn't sell or we didn't use.

I always had plenty of cream for whipping. I actually got sick of it sometimes we would have it so often. Every dessert would be "a la mode." I learned to use left over whipped cream by adding a pack of Jell-O to it and put it in the freezer to get frozen firm to eat like ice cream. Just think—today—that cream would be the same as "Half and Half". I would be a rich woman if I had that cream today. I learned that I could churn with my mixer, so I did that sometime when I was pushed for time. It was messy as it would splatter until I learned to cover it up. Later I bought myself a little hand churn that held about 1 ½ gallon at a time. I managed to save over $400.00 selling milk and butter.

I was saving that money to buy myself a new stove. I had seen it in a catalog and I had saved the picture until I could get the money. It was a stove that was an electric stove on one side and a wood cook stove on the other side. But to my dismay Bill wouldn't let me buy it. According to him we didn't need it. That was a disappointment to me as I had thought of nothing else. I wanted something modern like other people. I knew I would never get rid of that old wood stove. It was probably just as well as I never see a stove like that today. They must not have sold very well. But count it up—that was a lot of milk I sold!!!

In the summer, I always had canning and preserving of food to do. I canned blackberries first and from there it was non-stop until fall of the year after a frost. I made jelly, beet pickles, blackberries, green beans, cucumber pickles, grape juice, tomatoes, kraut, pickle beans, chow-chow, and peaches among a few. You name it I have canned it. I was even looking for a recipe to make tomato catsup. It all came in handy when the snow was on the ground and you couldn't get to town. I only tried to can corn one time as it would always spoil. It would take twice as long to can corn than anything. It was hard work but rewarding. Bill would bring his friends in and show them our can house and brag on it. I even learned to make pepper relish.

How many people today take the time to can?? Do they even want to learn? Do they even know how?? Should they learn??? Yes!!! It would help our food stamp program tremendously. There is no excuse for anyone to be without food. Just a little work is all that's needed.


# Kool Aid Ice Cream

Whip 2 cups of cream and make whipped cream. Sweeten to taste. Then add a package of your choice of Kool-Aid. Put it in an ice tray and place it in the freezer and freeze until firm. Makes good ice cream. Tastes good on a hot day. Also a way to keep from throwing out left over cream. And I definitely had left over whipped cream.

# Home Made Candy

Put: 2 cups of white sugar
1 cup of milk
2 tablespoons of Karo syrup
Dash of Salt
2 tablespoons of butter or margarine

Place everything in a cast iron skillet, if you have one, and put it on the stove and bring to a boil. Let it cook approximately 5 minutes at a hard boil until it starts looking dull. Test a teaspoon of the cooked mixture in a cup of cold water. Just drop a drop into the water and if it forms a soft ball it has cooked enough. Take it off the stove and begin stirring it until it starts to harden. Pour immediately into a buttered dish to continue to harden. Cut into squares when cool.

Variety to this: add 2 tablespoons of powdered cocoa to the first mix and cook as ordered. This will make chocolate candy.

After the mix cooks and is removed from the stove, add 1 cup of peanut butter in it and proceed to stir until set. This will make peanut butter fudge.

# Cottage Cheese

Skim cow's milk and put the cream into a jar to clabber or "set". This takes about 24 to 48 hours according to the weather. In summer it works faster. Just put this clabbered milk into a pan on the stove and let it get warm slowly. As the mixture gets hot it will cook and separate and curdle and become soft. After this happens pour off the watery liquid that is left and add fresh cream to the mix and salt to taste. It's as good as bought cottage cheese. The gimmick is to get the cow's milk.

# Signs

Every year we made a big garden and I canned what we didn't eat. It came in handy in the winter time. Cabbage was usually the first vegetable that was ready to eat. I fried cabbage and made slaw for as long as the cabbage was available. We loved to eat it raw with salt. I usually made kraut after we ate all the cabbage we could stand. It was cabbage every day for weeks. It would get so "ripe" I would have to do something with it or it would spoil. So—out comes my "crock."

I would always call my mom to see if the signs were right. After she had a stroke—one day I started to call her to ask her—and I remembered that she could no longer tell me. She was no longer able to tell me and I realized that I was on my own. It's an odd feeling to realize that now you are the next generation taking over. I did some "growing up" that day.

I made the "crock" full and it held about five gallons. I had to shred the cabbage and pack it in the crock. I then covered it with water—room temperature. If the water was too hot, the cabbage would rot and get soft. After I put the water in I covered it all with a layer of canning salt. I then wrapped a flat rock with a piece of thin white cloth and put this on top of the cabbage. I then put a cloth on the crock and secured it with a plate that .covered the top of the crock. This was put in a dark cool place to "work" or sour. After 10 days it would be ready. I could either can it or just leave it in the crock and get it straight from there when I wanted some to cook. I usually canned mine as I needed the crock for other things.

I also made pickle beans and chow -chow this same way. When you eat green beans in the summer until you can't face another one you make pickle beans. The same goes for corn. When you are tired of corn and beans both—you make chow-chow. It's made with cabbage, green beans and cut off corn. Make it just like kraut except you have to cook the beans until almost done and the corn has to be gotten hot. Let this all cool and mix with chopped cabbage and proceed as with kraut. Good eating in the cold winter months, with pork and corn bread.

I used my crock to make home-made wine from grapes. I usually just left it in the crock and used it from there. If you drink home-made wine too soon you get diarrhea. It was good to drink just a small amount before bed and you slept like a baby. It also calmed your stomach. It was a good tonic.

I canned several bushels of beans and then I would make dried beans or "shukey" beans. You did this by stringing and breaking the bean and then stringing them on a string with a needle and a strong piece of thread. They would be hung out to dry in the sun. If it rained they were brought in so they wouldn't get wet. If they did and it stayed damp for a few days then they would spoil by rotting or molding. After they were dried enough we put them in a sack and hung them up to use in the winter. It got to where they were hard to keep as bugs would find their way to them if you kept them too long. After freezers came along it was discovered that it was a good idea to put them in there.

I also dried applies for fried pies. You peeled and sliced them and laid them in the sun on a paper to dry. It was a constant chore as you had to watch to see if bees or bugs were getting on them. If the wind blew—it could blow your paper over and ruin all you hard work. It took several days of sunning to get them dry enough. It was at least a week or longer.

As you can see—farm wife's work is never done. One thing follows another. Then tomatoes are to be canned. Cucumbers made into pickles as are beets. Onions hung to dry also. Potatoes to gather and store, pears and apples also. A good storehouse for winter but also a lot of hard work. But educational work. Keeps you out of trouble.

# Gathering Wood

As we used wood stoves to cook and to keep the house warm we needed several loads of wood. We had an oil heater but where we lived that was just enough to knock the chill off of the house. In the winter the sun would shine for only a short time and it would be dark and cold again. We lived sandwiched between two mountains and we didn't get a lot of daylight because the sun would go behind the mountain and hide it and there went our sunshine and what little warmth a winter sun can give. I kept two stoves "hot" all winter plus an oil stove.

One year while the children were in school I went with my husband to gather wood. We borrowed a neighbor's flat bed sled and used our horse to pull it. We loaded an old apple tree he'd cut up earlier. We put it on the sled and here we come a pulling that sled of wood closer to the house from the field. It made me think I was a pioneer. It was some adventure. Did we ever stay warm that winter! Apple wood really warms your house.

If we ran out of wood, the boys had to help gather wood on Saturday when school was out or on days when they were home because of too much snow. They gathered wood in the snow the same as good weather. Their dad always took them the day before Christmas to buy their yearly boots. They always wore a toboggan, gloves and an old outdoor coat. They still got cold. Their noses would run and their eyes would water, how I hated that!. I felt like the wood should have been gathered when the weather was better. I couldn't say much as we needed it to keep warm.

I guess you've gathered by now we lived on a small farm that consisted of about 30 acres. We usually kept nine cows of which we milked one and sometime two or three at a time. We also had chickens, dogs and cats. We also raised tobacco. The money always came in handy at Christmas. I always saw that the children had a "big" Christmas. They always had a good Christmas as they weren't allowed toys except at Christmas so I made sure they got enough to last all year. Santa made sure of that.

# Water Pump

O ur water was pumped from a well by an electric pump. Well, one day a new house was being built up the road from us. The day they drilled their well our well went dry. For over two years I had to draw water with a bucket from the open well on our back porch. There was only a small amount of water in it. Not enough for the pump to pick it up. I used this water for cooking, drinking, washing out the milk strainer, and washing the dishes.

When I took a bath or washed my hair I had to go to the creek and carry the water home in a bucket until I got enough to fill the tub. I heated it on the wood stove. We couldn't drink water from the creek because, for starters, the cattle ran freely in the pasture and the creek. Also there were out-houses up the road from our house that spilt over into the ground water.

*This is what is left of the old well house. In the bottom was the well pump and shelves where I stored my canned goods and potatoes. This building was attached to the porch of the house and directly in front of the window was the hand dug well I mentioned. A door to the back of the upper part of the building led to the area where we used to raise little chickens and we stored onions here to dry in the fall after the chickens were gone. Inset: What is left of the old water pump. The tank is gone.*

You can guess that I had hair that was washed but not rinsed very well and it would look greasy. I wore it pulled back in a pony tail and it wasn't noticed as bad.

Finally my husband and a friend decided to dig the well deeper so we could use the pump again. It worked but then the pump started leaking. The water would run out onto the porch. One summer day there came a bad thunder and lighting storm and it set the pump on fire. Well — I had to walk over a board I had placed on the porch floor over the water to get to the switch to turn it off. It was forever getting "water logged" and would run all day if you didn't stop it. It would burn up the pump if I didn't turn it off and let it rest awhile. If I wanted water I would have to turn it back on. It was an old pump and hard to get parts for.

Our landlord didn't seem to mind our problem. I know there had to be an angel sitting on my shoulder when I lived in the country. I firmly believe it! If I hadn't have gotten electrocuted, my kids could have fallen in that open well. My daughter was born about this time so we had a diaper service to keep me in clean diapers. Getting the laundry done was something else.

My sister stayed with me for a few days when my daughter was born. She had a daughter that was a year older and still in diapers. It was embarrassing for her to have to try to bathe the child with my water situation as it was.

Everyone I knew had a TV but us. When my daughter was born my husband finally broke down and got us a second hand one. His sister was getting a new one and we bought her old one. It worked wonderfully for years. Of course the stations were limited as we lived surrounded by mountains and the stations couldn't be picked up.

See—no cable—just a dinky antenna. The only new thing I had in my house was a refrigerator. Everything else was second hand or hand me downs.

# Squirrel Hunting

My husband didn't like to fish or deer hunt but he did like to go squirrel hunting and run rabbit dogs and hunt rabbits. One day he was off from work and decided to take me squirrel hunting. We

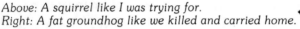

*Above: A squirrel like I was trying for.*
*Right: A fat groundhog like we killed and carried home.*

started out right after we did the outside work of milking and feeding the pigs. The bus had just picked up the children and they would be in school all day.

We climbed up the hill to the top of the ridge above the back of the house, through the pasture. We could see everywhere from up there. We rested a while and then decided to move on as we hadn't seen any squirrels. We walked and walked the hills when we finally sighted one in a tree on a limb.

They will run if they hear you or see you so you have to walk very quietly. You could just barely see the squirrel as it was partly behind the trunk of the tree. Bill gave me the gun and showed me how to use it. He told me to shoot near the neck if I could so the head and body wouldn't be bruised and bloody. He liked to eat the brains of a squirrel after they were boiled. Well—I shot and totally missed the squirrel. I shot again and again—about five times. It finally fell to the ground. I had shot that poor squirrel to pieces. Of course, it wasn't fit to eat.

So off we go again. We walked and walked—all day to be exact! The squirrels weren't out that day as we failed to see anymore. We found the foundation of an old house that had burned down. It looked like an old cabin and it looked like it had burned down a long time ago. The chimney was still standing and there were flowers growing where it looked like the door had been. Walking home we sighted a groundhog eating. Bill shot it. We had to carry it home. It felt like it weighed 50 pounds. We took turns carrying it. When we got home we were starved as we hadn't eaten since leaving home in the morning.

When we got home the kids were getting off of the school bus. We had been gone all day. We rested a while and then he skinned the groundhog. I had to put it in my refrigerator freezer as I didn't have a regular freezer. I couldn't buy ice cream for months as there was no room for it. The groundhog took up all of my freezer space. One day I finally cooked it. Boy, did it stink! It ruined the pot I parboiled it in. I didn't eat a bite of it. It was an experience to kill it but eating it was something else. Groundhogs are supposed to be clean. So I'm told they just eat from plants and berries and fruits and green grass and plants. They are vegetarians. They won't eat old meat like some wild animals.

Bill used to squirrel hunt a lot and always killed at least five to ten at a hunting. We didn't kill any the day I went because the ground was dry and the leaves crackled when you walked on them scaring them. You went squirrel hunting when the ground was damp after a snow or rain. Of course, I ended up cleaning the squirrels he killed because he would sit down in his easy chair to rest and read the paper and the next thing you knew he was sound asleep. I couldn't leave them until morning, they would spoil and I would be in trouble. Squirrels didn't smell bad when being cleaned but rabbits stunk something awful.

# Crows

We had a lot of crows in the country. They would pull up your corn the minute it came through the earth while it was tender. It would be just beginning to sprout. We would have to replant several times to get a good full row, or a good "stand" as it was referred to.

I remember when my husband worked graveyard. I would have to get up at 4 o'clock in the morning and watch for the crows. They always did their dirty work while everyone was asleep. It was always early, right before daylight.

One of the crows would sit on a post at the garden and be a watchdog for the other crows. If anything moved he would "squawk" and alert the ones in the garden eating. If I tried to open the screen door to ease my rifle to where I could shoot—they would hear it and they would all fly away and watch to when they could come back.

I learned to crack the door and prop it open with something so I wouldn't have to touch it. I got up every day for a week to do this until the corn grew enough so they wouldn't touch it. After it got so big they wouldn't eat it. You've heard the old saying "you can hear corn growing at night, it grows so fast". If the crows got at that corn I was in trouble.

Bill used to take the boys crow hunting late in the day. Their nests are very high in a tree. You had to climb up to get the little crows before they could fly. It's hard to get an adult crow as they are very smart.

We had one as a pet one time. It messed everywhere on the back porch that was closed in. It would squawk very loudly in the morning when I came into the kitchen to build a fire. It got on my nerves something awful. It would squawk until I fed it. I hated to have to feed it before I could feed my family. Bill finally killed it and used it as a decoy to scare off other-crows. A saying goes that they won't come around a garden where there hangs a dead crow.

# Church-Country

I went to church every Sunday with my children. My husband never went but he wanted us to go. He had a bad experience as a child from a teacher and he would not go back after he was grown. He wanted his children dressed decent and them well fed. I guess, because his dad died when Bill was just a baby and they had a hard time.

I always wore gloves over my hands to church because they always looked so bad. They were always stained or rough looking from work. In town, I wore fingernail polish and was proud of my hands. I wouldn't let my daughter hoe in the garden or the corn field. I didn't want her hands to look like mine.

I helped with church bazaars sometimes, until my husband told me I couldn't do it anymore. I was needed at home. Our booth always sold more than the other ones. I took candy, pies, cupcakes and cakes to sell.

Our only car was a 1950 Ford pickup truck—all four of the children and myself piled into it and off to church we went. He later bought me a used car to drive when he took the truck to work.

When the children got old enough to "cut up" in church I had to get stern with them. After a few Sundays of calling them down as

*Left: Plain's Methodist Church. Right: Easter Photo—in front, David, Cindy, and me. Back row: John and Jim.*

they just kept on, I promptly got up and ushered them out of the church and to the truck with the destination being home. Parents usually just took them outside and scolded them and brought them back in. Well—I had four and it was a little harder to discipline them there. I was so "mad" and embarrassed too that I didn't say a word going home and it only took me about five minutes to get there.

They knew they were in trouble and so were very quiet also. I told them to stay in the barn until I got back. I got a little "keen switch" and switched their legs and back through their clothes. There was more racket than pain but just the action was enough. My husband was in bed sleeping after working graveyard the night before. He wanted to know why I was home so early as he had heard us drive up in the truck. After I explained what had happened he said "Well, your mom's already punished you so I won't, but I should." They were good after that. They started sitting separate after that to keep from being tempted to "cut up" again. Of course, David, the baby talked a lot and his Sunday School teacher made him sit on a stool in front of the room. I didn't know this for some time. The teacher had gotten to where when he came in she just made him sit up there before he even did anything. I noticed he didn't like to go as well as he used to. He got to where he didn't like to go in the morning but he liked going at night to the youth programs. There was a different teacher at night. I was a little upset with this lady to say the least. It would be better to have a child in church even if he was a little restless than not to be there at all.

# Children, Swimming Hole & Snakes

My husband's family all learned to swim in the creek in the "water hole" by the big walnut tree. One day I decided to go down and watch my children swimming. I could hear them yelling and having fun.

They were taught to swim by being thrown in (and get out the best you can) or else go to the YMCA in town and learn there. Our two older boys got thrown in but the two younger children learned at the "Y". They all got to swim at the "Y" but days they didn't go there they swam in their own private swimming hole.

To get to the swimming hole you had to go through a field with grass about waist high. We were letting it grow to make hay for our cattle. It was difficult to walk through, so I proceeded to hop through it. I was about half way to the pond when I jumped up in the grass starting to put my foot down, when what was before me but a large flattened out area. There in the middle of it lay several snakes. I didn't stop to count them but I knew there was more than one. They were just lying there in the sun. I stopped in mid-air and did a quick turnaround and headed back to the house. I forgot all about watching

*Our house was to the right side of the picture, across the road and on the hill. "X" marks the snake nest. The arrow points to the swimming hole below the walnut tree.*

the kids swim. I had to let my heart quit racing. The children came home a different way, by the trail that I should have taken.

# Outhouse

When I first moved to the country, we had no indoor bath facilities. If we needed to go to the bathroom we had to go outside to the outhouse. It sat out to the right of the house. You could see it from one of the windows.

Bill was always "pranking" people. One day he saw a boy that lived up the road from them. He was walking up the road one day and decided he needed to go to the bathroom before he got home. So—he just came through our yard and into the outhouse he went. Bill waited a few minutes and then he got his gun. He aimed for the roof of the building. You could hear the sound of the bullet hitting the tin roof. Nothing happened. He fired again. All of a sudden the door of the outhouse came open and out came the boy yelling "Dad-gum it Bill, Stop!!" his pants were down to his knees and he was pulling on them trying to get them up. They were his buddies—so no harm done. After about a year a bathroom was put in the house.

# Sour-Kraut

In the early part of the Spring into Summer our cabbage would be ready to eat. It is usually planted all at one time and therefore it is ready to eat all at the same time. I would cook it about every way I could think of but we still had cabbage that would need to be put up for the winter.

I would make sour-kraut. To do this you have to grate the cabbage and put it in a clean crock. Do not use soap in the crock before making the kraut. You fill the crock nearly full. To this you put cool water, not cold. If the water is too hot it will cook the cabbage and it will spoil. You then add about ½ cup of pickling salt, not table salt. There is a difference! Sprinkle this over the top of the cabbage. You then wrap a flat rock with a clean white cloth—still no soap. It is best to use new cheese cloth. This helps to keep the cabbage from rising in the jar. Next cover the whole crock with cheese cloth and secure it so it won't come off. Place the crock in a dark cool place to let it "work". It takes about ten days to two weeks. It is then ready to heat and place in jars to seal. You can leave it in the crock if the crock isn't needed for something else.

There are pickled beans that require a crock and also pickled corn. Also in the fall when the grapes are ready to harvest, you may want to make a crock of home made wine. A good tonic and it helps you to sleep. If you drink it too soon, however, you will get a royal belly ache and diarrhea.

Sometimes I would have to empty jars of kraut I had made the year before to have jars to can in. One day I was doing this and after about six to eight jars being dumped out under the apple tree — I was shocked to see what I had dumped out crawling with the biggest worms. I almost dropped the jar I was getting ready to empty. I got the willy's and ran back to the house. I thought "were those in the jars I had just emptied or where did they come from? I looked the other jars I had left unopened and there were no worms there. Those worms had to have come out of the ground when I poured that sour-kraut out. They couldn't stand the sour juice and they came to the surface for air and survival. To this day I don't like kraut and every time it's mentioned I see those worms. I never told anyone as I didn't want to turn them against sour- kraut.

# New Couch

Soon after my second son was born, my mother-in-law moved to town to be closer to her job. She did not work the same shift as Bill anymore and it was difficult to get to work sometimes. She would have to walk aways down the road to meet the work bus. This was hard when it rained or the weather turned cold. She caught a ride sometime with a lady that lived up the road from us but sometimes the lady would go into town early and then Hattie would have to hurry to try to catch the bus.

When she moved she took part of her furniture. So this in turn made us have to go furniture buying. I did get a new refrigerator out of the deal. Every thing else was second hand.

While the children were in school one day and Bill was off from work, we went to Asheville to shop for a couch. We went to Pearlman's and several other furniture stores. Furniture buying is about as bad as car buying. The prices looked rather high but I was having a good time looking at furniture and wishing. After they showed us all their couches, we couldn't decide which one to take. I would have been happy with either one as long as it was new. Then Bill speaks up and asks to see the second hand living room sets. My heart sank—Oh No!!—someone else's left overs. They took us to this dark and dreary room full of old furniture.

Sure enough, that is what we ended up with. I was so disappointed. Bill's reasoning was that we would get a better one when the children were older. They'll just tear up a new one. Talk about being embarrassed when the children's teachers came to the house to visit the parents. There was one teacher that did this with each child. She thought it would help the child's learning if the parents and teachers were friendly with each other. It might have worked as my children did make good grades in school. Back to the couch!! With the couch was a chair that went with it. So we took it too. It was a swivel chair or a chair that would rock back and forth or would turn completely around with the base not moving. It was a good couch, construction wise. It was very heavy and the arms felt like they had metal in them.

One night Bill had gone to work on the night shift and I had gotten the children to bed. I was still up as I never got to bed when everyone else did. I always had chores to do as the old saying goes "a women's work is never done." I was either canning something, ironing or peeling potatoes to fry for breakfast with country ham or sausage. Anyway, as I reached to pull the string on the light overhead in the living room, the dumb cord just broke right off in my hand. I couldn't reach the bulb to twist it so the light would go out. I couldn't let it burn all night. I began to look around for something to stand on. What did I stand on but that stupid swivel chair as it was closest to the light. Right when I took a hold of the bulb to twist it, that hateful chair swirled around and threw me onto the arm of it. It felt like lead it was so hard. It almost knocked me out as I saw stars and did it ever hurt!! It knocked the breath out of me so bad that all I could do was sit there a few minutes. I tried to get up to walk but was too dizzy. Of course, everyone was asleep and I knew Bill wouldn't be home until after seven in the morning. I had to get to the bed—I had to bend over to walk as I couldn't stand up—my side hurt so bad. I managed to get to the bed and lay there a while . I finally went to sleep as I was tired. As I had gotten the light turned off it was pitch dark in the house.

In the country there were no outside lights like there are in town. In town the light was right at my bedroom window and shown in keeping the room "lit" up all night. After about a week when my side didn't get better, I went to the doctor. After x-rays it was found that I had four fractured ribs. I was given a binder to wear until it got better. It took about a year for it to finally quit bothering me. I was not relieved of any of my chores either. They were still there for me to do.

We only paid about $100.00 for the couch and chair and it lasted until my husband died. I had covered it with a clear plastic cover and it looked almost as it did the day we bought it. I could have had a new couch after all. My children were not destructive with furniture, mostly I guess, because they stayed outside most of the time playing. When I see young people today getting new furniture, I think back to when all I ever had was second-hand or hand-me-downs that had already been used. Times change!!!! I wonder. Is it for the better? If kids today started out with a few hand me downs they may not be in debt so.

# Dogs

There was a man my husband worked with that kept beagle dogs to hunt rabbits with. He got my husband interested in them too. He started out with a female he called "Jody", after me. I'm still trying to decide if that was a compliment or not! The male he called "Smokey". He was a little short legged beagle and he was a beagle all the way. He got another dog he called "Cindy" after our daughter. So I guess one being named after me was probably all right as he thought the world of the daughter. She was the only girl in a family of three boys.

We ended up with between eight and ten beagles at a time. I had to feed them and keep water for them. They were chained to a dog house individually. When it rained it never failed that one of them would get its chain caught on the nail that held the chain to the house. It would bark until I released it. I kept a pair of rubber boots with a pair of loafers in them to wear when I had to do farm work. I kept them on the back porch so they were handy when I needed them. The dog getting its chain caught almost always happened in the night when my husband was at work. So out I went into the dark in my gown and a rain coat to help the dog. I had to do it because it's barking might disturb the neighbors and the children.

One summer when chained out of the sun up in the woods behind the house, I had to get up in the night and help them . It was on a hill that went straight up. Here I am in the middle of the night climbing this hill with a flashlight trying to shut up these dogs. I had to or I wouldn't have gotten any sleep. Beagles are very loud and insistent.

I fed them by cooking a big cake of cornbread in a big pan. I cooked it in the wood stove from fresh ground cornmeal. No self -rising corn meal for us. I should be so lucky! I would have used it in a minute but my husband believed in everything being as fresh as possible without preservatives. I mixed it up with fresh cow's milk. They also got some dry food but mostly they got that during hunting season. I mean I had this bread to bake every day. How many today would do that?

I was in deep trouble if a good running dog got "with pups" and couldn't run when rabbit season started in the fall. My job was to keep the females up during "heat". I put them in the top of the barn loft. One day I had to knock a male dog off of the ladder leading to the loft. The ladder was straight up but that dog had almost climbed it to the top. I had to take the ladder down and put it back only when I needed to feed them to prevent possible intruders. I was very successful and prevented any dogs from not being able to run.

On Bill's day off he would take the dogs about dark to the woods to let them run. I had to let them be a little hungry so they wouldn't be lazy and not run. They had to be a little hungry to chase a rabbit or the scent of where the rabbit had been. The only bad part, was that he took them in hearing distance of the house. I lay there all night and heard those dogs run until daylight, barking and howling all the time. They would get extremely loud if they got on the scent of a rabbit. He would usually take our boys whether they wanted to go or not. We did enjoy the beagle pups when we had them. The kids loved to play with them.

# Rats

R ats were abundant in the country, both big and small. This was so because we had corn cribs full of corn and cow feed we kept in a big barrel. Sometimes the boys would not get the lid on tight and the rats could get down in it. Also as long as we had a pig to feed the rats would hang around their pen to get what spilled over the rim of the pig trough.

When we opened the door to the corn crib, mice would run everywhere. We would open it sometimes just to see them run.

There were "Wharf Rats" also. These are very large rats, some as big as a kitten. We had a bucket that we kept right outside the kitchen door on the screened-in porch. We put scraps and milk in it for the pigs. I poured out sometimes as much as two gallons of milk at a time. I would get so much milk in the refrigerator that I would have to throw out some to make room for the fresher milk. At night the "wharf rats" would make their way to the porch and make a mess especially if anything was left in the bucket overnight. The rats could get onto the porch by squeezing through a small area where the porch was attached to a rock wall. It would be worse in the winter.

I went to town and bought five "wharf rat" traps. At night after the children were put to bed and it was quiet I would set the traps. Rats don't come out very much in daylight hours. The first night that I set those traps, I caught at least six rats, one right behind the other. As soon as the trap would 'throw", I would wait a few minutes until the rat had time to die and stop moving. Then I would go to the porch and release them from the trap and reset it. One time I let the rat go too soon and it got up and ran away. So I learned to wait until I was sure that it was dead. I would tie a piece of fat back with a thread to the trap to catch them and they were caught so fast, they didn't get a bite of it.

# Worst Birthday

I went to visit my parents after my birthday once. They didn't have a car and didn't visit us often. It was already after my birthday and I didn't go just to get a gift. I am not a person used to getting a lot of attention on my birthday so it had not entered my mind that there was a gift for me.

Anyway—I was given a "used quilt." The reason I was given the old quilt was that the kids would tear up a good one pulling at it the way children will. I was told when the kids got older I could have a new one.

It didn't set too well with me as it was very well worn. I cried all the way home about it. I had just as soon as not gotten a quilt at all. I kind of had a feeling that people looked down on me anyway. Referring to the country sometimes made you think people thought you were a "country hick". In other words, "not as good as the people in town". I didn't have many modern conveniences like people in town so I guess I felt that way really. It just made me more determined that I'd make it on my own some way. I feel I accomplished my goal but really I don't care either way.

# Best Birthday

Another year for my birthday I was given a brand new pressure cooker. I had been canning with a two piece enamel canner and it took a long time to can with it. It took four hours with the old canner to can green beans. It would take all afternoon. It only took about 15-20 minutes in my new canner. I really did appreciate it and used it for years. Those days are gone forever. When my children were all grown my life changed and was not so hard. Feeding six hungry mouths takes a lot of food, a lot of time and a lot of dishwashing.

# Flu Epidemic

There was a flu epidemic when all my children were small. It must have been in the mid-50's. My husband was given a flu shot at work and a few days later he came down with the flu. I mean in a bad way. His temperature went up and he was in the bed for over a week. It started out with him and extended to the whole family but me. I was the only one on foot for days. I called the family doctor to come to treat them. I waited all day. I had given up on him when in the night about midnight, I heard a knock on the door and there stood the doctor. He looked very tired. He said, "I've been making house calls all day for the flu." Canton was full of it. I remember their fever was high, they couldn't eat and just laid in bed. Somehow it escaped me. I guess the Lord saved me to take care of the farm and the sick. Bill missed over a week from work.

# Big Snows

In the fifties we had snows that hung around for a while. It would snow and then turn bitter cold. The snow would freeze on top of the ground making it slow to melt. One snow stayed so long that I did not get out of the cove for over two weeks. As long as there was any snow on the road I wasn't allowed to drive the car. Bill drove an old "fliver" he used for work. No one took good cars to the mill because of the fallout. It would settle on the car and eat the paint off of the vehicle. He went to work but I wasn't allowed out during bad weather. I really couldn't go anyway as the children were home during snow storms.

I kept two wood burning stoves going 24 hours a day during cold weather. We also had an oil heater but it didn't give off enough heat for the whole house. We kept the wood on the enclosed back porch to keep it dry. Frozen water pipes were a problem. I had a little oil lantern that I kept under our house near the pipes to keep them from freezing. I had to get down on my hands and knees to put it under the house through a little opening. It had to be away from the wind or it would blow it out. This worked very well. I had to take it out in the morning when I got up and then again at night. It had to be refilled at least twice a day as it didn't hold very much.

Our fields would freeze over and the children with all the neighbor children would skate on it. When they would tire of that they would sleigh ride. They used anything they could find. I looked out and two of them were sailing across the field sitting in my old "washing machine lid". They were heading straight for the creek. Of course, it was partly frozen over too. They used old pieces of card board boxes and we had one sled. They would fight over who got it.

I always kept two pair of pants that I wore to do the chores. Yes, I wore two pair at one time, one over the other. I also had a pair of rubber boots that I kept a pair of loafers in to wear outside. I wore those boots summer or winter. I never left the house without having them on. I never knew what I might come across and need protection. When you have dogs to feed, pigs to feed, eggs to gather from the nests, milking to do you just might run into a snake, a mud hole, high weeds and a creek to cross. I wore a scarf around my neck and I never got cold, no matter how cold it got. Those boots lasted close to twenty years.

# Christmas Trees

L iving in the country has it's advantages. Everything is plentiful. You just have to learn to use and take care of it. We never had to buy a Christmas tree. When the boys were old enough to walk they went with their dad Christmas tree hunting. After they brought it home it was cut to size and a piece of wood was nailed to the bottom so it would stand up level.

After the boys got big enough, they would get anxious and go by themselves, if their dad was working and couldn't get to it. They learned to nail the board on it as they had been shown. The tree always stood as straight as an arrow. The good thing about getting the tree in the country, it was free. You just had to walk in the woods until you found the one you wanted. No one ever said anything to you if you were on their land. The reason being, they may want a tree on your land. We always had a cut tree. We never dug one up, it was too heavy to carry.

Santa was always good to my children because it was the only time of the year that they got a new toy. They were too busy playing outside or working.

One year my older brother came out to look for a tree. Bill was working graveyard and was sleeping so the boys went with them. They walked in the woods but did not find one suitable. He had brought his new wife with him. He liked the country even though he was raised in town like me. He lived in an apartment down the road from us for about a year.

# Big Meals

Having a big family of four and with a hungry man I cooked a lot, especially when school was out. No poor eaters at my house. I don't remember anyone ever turning their noses up at food like kids do today. I baked bread every day and a dessert every day—as it was always eaten. For breakfast I would cook either ham, bacon or sausage from the pigs we raised. There was usually a big pan of fresh liver mush to fry or to make sandwiches with. We usually canned the sausage and cured the hams and bacon with salt. We never had beef—just pork and fish sometimes. The chicken we had were raised and killed and dressed at home. How I hated those bantie chickens. They were always tough.

For breakfast I would have ham and fried potatoes with fresh cooked applesauce. We always ate applesauce with pork. The night before I would peel potatoes to fry for breakfast. It would equal a five pound bag you buy at the store today. The kids ate every bite and fought over the pan to get the last bite. We always raised about twenty bushels of potatoes in our garden for the winter. We always ate home grown food. Only staples as coffee, sugar and flour were bought from a store.

One day when my husband was going to the store I gave him a list of things I wanted. My mouth was watering for a banana pudding. I asked for vanilla wafers, bananas and pudding mix. Well—he comes back with a bunch of bananas. I asked where the other things were and he said "We have eggs, milk and flour, you can make the vanilla wafers . We have milk and eggs and flour, you can make the pudding." Well—forget the banana pudding! I don't remember even thinking banana pudding again after that for I knew the reply I would get. Did I make the pudding? No!

As you can gather we usually had a lot of fresh fruit pies. I always put up in jars plenty of blackberries that my husband and the children picked. We always had plenty of apples. You can be well fed in the country but you have to work a little. You pick it yourself instead of standing in line at the check out counter at the grocery store.

# Spoiled Peaches

One summer Bill went to South Carolina with a friend. When they came home they asked me for a bushel basket. I had no idea what they wanted it for. They opened the trunk of the car and it was full of peaches. They had gotten them for 50 cents a bushel and there were about six bushels of them. They took out 2 bushels for me and divided the rest with the other two men for their wives.

These peaches had been dead ripe when they got them. They said they didn't get baskets for them because they would have cost more than the peaches. The heat in the trunk had really "worked" on them. They were almost beyond saving. I think I got about 5 quarts and a pie out of mine. I should have gotten about 30 quarts instead. What a mess it was!!! They had just dumped the peaches in the trunk without anything under them. I bet the man that owned that car had a time getting the smell of those soured peaches out of there. Were those few peaches we salvaged worth it???

# Planting Beans

After school was out one summer a boy came to visit with Ada, my next door neighbor. He played with my boys during the day. One day Bill had left orders that the boys were to plant corn field beans by the corn that had already come up. As they grew they would climb the corn. They planted like they were told with about 2 to 3 to a stalk.

The visiting boy had to go home after lunch and he wanted to play in the creek one more time before he had to leave. Someone came up with the idea to put more than 2-3 beans at a time. So they started putting several beans at a time to get rid of them sooner. They finished and went to the creek and played as planned.

About ten days later Bill was hoeing the corn and looking for the beans to come up. After school, he took the boys to the garden and showed them their handiwork. There were clumps of beans in one place and hardly any other places. He gave them a good talking to and told them "that their sins will find you out."

# Shooting

We never lacked for something to do to keep us entertained. One day out came the 22 rifle to be cleaned. After Bill cleaned it we took turns, children and all, trying to shoot cans off of the fence posts in front of our house, across the road. The children put them back up as we shot them off. They always stayed on the porch with us until we stopped shooting before they picked the cans up. I was pretty good as I rarely missed the can—over it went every time. They used to kid Bill and tell him he had better not make me mad or I'd shoot him. Of course, they followed this with laughter. The children were pretty good "shots" too. The front porch was a good place to shoot from as there was nothing but a pasture we shot toward and we could see if anything was in the way. We would do this for a couple of hours. The boys however did not show a great deal of interest in guns or hunting, as time went on.

# School Clothes

I had four children in school at the same time. Before school started in the fall I went to town and bought all the children five changes of clothes. One for each day of the week. I only let them wear them one time before I washed them. Every day I ironed their clothes for the next day and hung them on the back of a door. I had a rod on it that was strong enough to hold them all. When it was pushed back you couldn't see the clothes. They were there handy if we got up late. Houses didn't have many closets then if any. I look back and wonder where we kept our clothes. Our house only had two small ones.

# Grass Fire

One Spring, Bill's cousin was clearing some pasture that be longed to an aunt. They had been burning brush, when they decided to stop and go to the house and eat their lunch. I was in our front yard when I saw some dry grass across the fence in the neighbor's pasture start to burn. It was brown dead grass and the flame was going over the ground like wild fire. Out come those men from the house running as fast as they could straight up that hill. They started beating it out with anything they could get their hands on. They had to climb the fence to get to it. It burned about an acre of land before they got it stopped. They got it stopped short of the woods it was heading for. It was a close call for sure.

# Tree House

Bill let a neighbor make a tree house in our woods one year. He was the same age as my children and they played with him. He was an only child. They even had a stove in it.

One day I had gone to town and when I came home there was a fire truck in the road over from the woods. Bill was at work. Smoke was billowing everywhere. They got the fire out without it hurting the woods. Bill's uncle had noticed the smoke and called the fire department and I am glad he did. If I had of been home I still wouldn't have seen the smoke because it was around a curve from our house. Children and matches don't go together. David said that they had built a big fire and left the stove door open.

# Cow Chase

New calves were being born at all times of the year. When one was born one of us usually went to check on it. We needed to see if the cow had expelled the afterbirth and to see if the calf was up and had nursed. A calf needs to be on its feet and nursing soon thereafter, usually within 30 minutes.

One morning I was the only one at home when I noticed a new calf with it's mother in the lower pasture. It looked like I might need to milk her as her "bag" was full and she was our milk cow. I got my bucket and went through the pasture to where she was. She was in the edge of the woods on a slight hill. Every time I started to get close to her, she would bow her head, horns and all and run at me. By the way, her name was "Horny". I tried several times to get close to her and I just finally just gave up. She was snorting like a bull and really acted like one. I didn't press the issue as I didn't want to get "gored".

# Snake Bite

I had always heard that a black snake wouldn't bite you. Their job was to kill other snakes and mice. They were supposed to be a "good" snake. One summer Bill and some boys found a black snake. They caught it and put it in a "burlap sack". He was going to bring it home to put in our barn loft to kill rats. He got the snake in the sack all right but when he went to move the sack the snake struck at the sack and bit Bill on his finger. He said it was hanging on for dear life. His finger bleed from it. He had no reaction from it. Just a sore thumb for a few days. After he put it in the loft I wouldn't gather eggs from the hen nests anymore. The chickens had nests in the hay in the barn loft. I never saw the snake so I believe it left the country anyway.

# Gathering Eggs

If you have never found a nest full of hen eggs you don't know what you have missed. When you come upon a nest full of eggs you feel as good as if you had found a million dollars. All enjoyments in life don't have to cost a lot of money. Country life is something everyone should experience at least once. So many surprises.

# New Calf

We had a young cow that got pregnant earlier than we wanted her too. We usually wanted them to be at least two years old. This one was expecting by the time she was that old. It's hard to keep up with all of them. Anyway, I watched her when I thought the calf was due. I would walk the pasture looking for her if she wasn't with the others. One day I found her by the branch with her new calf. Yes, another calf born by the creek. This calf was nearly as big as she was. She had cleaned up and was going about her business as though nothing had happened. The calf was running around as healthy as could be. Was I surprised. I was afraid she couldn't have the calf as she was just a calf herself.

# Lilies

D own the road from our house was a big curve. On down the road from this curve grew the prettiest orange lilies. They bordered the road and were over knee high. They grew wild and came back every fall. The children would gather them and bring them home for a flower pot for me. Jim was the one who liked flowers best. He was forever bringing me wildflowers for the table. I didn't have time to grow tame flowers.

# Wood Fire

B ill cleared the pine thicket he had taken me through to go blackberry picking that time. The land belonged to his Aunt and she told him he could pasture it if he would clear it off. He cut and worked there every chance he got, on his days off, and even would work there after work. He was trying to get it ready to pasture for the summer. After he got it cleared, it had to be burned to get it off the ground. One morning, he was working 3-11 and decided he was going to burn it before he went to work. He went to each pile of brush and cut down pine trees and set them all on fire. This was a mistake. When it was time for him to go to work, it was still burning.

The Fire Warden on Mt. Pisgah sighted it and reported it to the town fire department. They came to see about it. Here comes a big fire truck up the road on this little country road. Something to see! They told him that he couldn't leave it until it was almost out. So I had to call the mill and tell them he would be late to work. He didn't get to go to work until 6 o'clock and the fire was still smoldering.

He got to use the pasture for a few years before she decided she wanted it for her own use. There could have been "rich pine" in it that made it burn so big and so long. It looked like the whole mountain was on fire.

# Sunday Paper

Three times a month on Sunday morning before anyone got up, I got to go to town to pick up the Sunday paper from the paper stand in front of one of the grocery stores. When Bill worked he would bring it home with him, but when he was off, I went for it. I usually got up and just went in my robe and gown and bed slippers.

One morning I saw something that weaned me of that habit. I was riding along and noticed this truck by the road and a young girl with a man standing looking at the front of her truck. The wheels had just come off of that truck and rolled out from under it and the front of the truck was on the ground.

From then on I dressed in street clothes before my trip to town. This included good walking shoes too. Wouldn't I have been a pretty thing in my bed slippers and gown on the side of the road?

# Cloud Burst

In June of 1963, an unusual storm hit the Willis Cove where we lived. One afternoon dark clouds formed quickly and everything got dark and impending rain was evident. I got the children in the house. Their dad was sleeping as he was working the night shift again. The rain started and it got heavier and was coming down very hard. We hear a roar and noticed the creek getting "out of it's banks".

It was the water coming down from upstream. It only rained about an hour but when it was over, our bottom land in front of the house was flooded to the point of looking like a lake. We saw a bird sitting on top of the pig pen and luckily the pen didn't wash away. I bet those pigs got a scare when their pen filled half full of water.

Old Timers refer to this as a "Cloud Burst". It happened so fast, Bill didn't even know the bottom land was flooded. He thought it was just raining. He was surprised when he got up to see the water all over. When he came home from work the next morning, he said that we were the only area affected by the storm. Everywhere else everyone had sunshine all day without a cloud. It had not rained in town or up the other cove from us.

It was scary to see especially as it happened so fast. There was a large man-made lake located on a mountain off of Newfound Road. This was in the general direction that the storm seemed to have come from. This same dam burst several years later and flooded several homes located below it toward Asheville.

# Conclusion

In 1968, Bill died as the result of a cerebral hemorrhage at the age of 40. As the farm belonged to his mother, I used the proceeds from a small insurance policy to buy a home for myself and the children. I knew I would at least have a roof over our head if nothing else.

I was so used to having cattle and a garden that I bought a place with three acres of land and a pasture with a barn. I could keep a milk cow and make a garden. I guess this had been instilled in me by Bill that I just couldn't let go—not yet. I kept the cow in this pasture and also made a garden that I shared with my neighbors.

It showed out when it came to squash. I furnished squash to anyone of my neighbors who wanted it. I even sold milk awhile. I kept the other cows we owned out in the country where we owned some land. The land had been bought with money I had saved for a house of our own. I had to give up the money to buy the land during an auction near where we lived one Saturday. It was such a good deal and it joined the farm we lived on.

When the boys went off to college I sold the cow I had near our house. I kept the ones in the country for several years. One of them started getting out and tearing down the fence, so I just sold them all as I didn't have anyone to help me to repair the fence. There were about nine of them as I recall. I took hay to them everyday in the winter. They knew my car and met me at the fence sometimes. Other times I had to carry it across the creek and up the hill through the woods to the shed. It was a job. Especially, every day. In the summer they were no problem.

I had my cows artificially bred and it got to be a lot of trouble with that. I kept the calf until it was about six weeks old and then sell it. It brought more money at that age than when they were older. I didn't miss them after I sold them. They are a good hobby and it keeps you out of trouble.

By our living so "close to the land" we had managed to save enough money to pay for our first child's education but with little to spare. He in turn sent home money after he went into the Marines after college. Jim went to college with the help of a scholarship from Champion and his working to help defray the rest of the cost. Cindy went to St. Genevive's School for secretaries and David had help from Social Security for his education.

I did enjoy my life in the country and I feel that anyone who hasn't had the experience is really missing something. It is entirely different from town living. You are so close to nature and God's creation.

# IV.

# REMEMBERING FAMILY

# My Children

John was my first born. He was born a week before my birthday on January 14, 1950. He was born six weeks premature and weighed only 4 lb. 12 oz. He had no fingernails or eyelashes. He had no hair on his body except a little fuzz at the back of his head. He stayed in the hospital until he weighed 5 lbs. That was the required weight for a new born before he could be discharged. It cost a total of $30.00 for the time he spent in the hospital after I went home. As he stayed 30 days it cost $1. per day. Can you believe it???

James (Jim) was the second child and he was born about a week before the due date. He weighed 6 lb. 14 oz. He was born on a late Easter night—really early in the morning on Monday. He was very dark in color. He was a breech birth that could have accounted for the dark color. The umbilical cord was around his neck several times.

When they told me it was a boy—I cried—I had sort of hoped it would be a girl since I already had a boy. That's just the way of human nature. When the nurse brought him in for me to see, I fell in love with him immediately. He was such a pretty baby. To heck with a girl—I'll have one later.

He was born 14 months after John. I really had my hands full. I hadn't got over having had John—so of course, I was a little run down. When I got up to the bathroom, I fainted dead away in the floor. The nurses dared me to lock the bathroom door because if I fainted again—they wouldn't be able to get to me.

I had two babies in diapers at the same time. I had to wean Jim from his bottle at nine months old because John kept stealing Jim's bottle. I tried to wean him when he was two years old but it wasn't easy because he could see Jim's bottle and would take it away from him. Jim was also weaned from his diaper at an earlier age than most. He walked at 1 year of age. John wasn't walking when Jim was born. He was 18 months old before he walked.

Cindy was third and the only child born that I didn't have complications with. Instead of being born early, she was born 2 weeks past her due date. I was in labor only 4 hours. She was my biggest baby as she weighed 7 lb. 7 ½ oz. When she was born the nurse's teased the doctor. She said "this is the third red head you have delivered this week." He was red headed. Of course, it was a joke!! Cindy's red hair came from her Grandma Wood.

David was last and also born 1 month early. He weighed 5 lb. 3 ½ oz. and was born on his Grandmother's birthday. (His Daddy's Mother—Hattie). He had to have fluid taken from his lungs. He and John both had to have this because they were premature.

When he was 18 months old he had a bad case of croup. He had to be under an oxygen tent for several days and also had an emergency "trach" inserted in his throat. We had private nurses with him for 10 days. He was one sick baby. He was weaned from his bottle when he got sick but that's all we could get him to take, so we had to give it back to him.

John Wood born 1/14/ 50      Jim Wood born 3/26/51
Cindy Wood 12/25/53       David Wood 2/23/56

I went into shock after David was born and had to have four units of blood. The nurse had put me on the bedpan and had left the room. When she came back in I was falling to the floor and she grabbed me before I completely fell. She had left the rail down on the bed and

*David—Jim—Cindy—John*

there was nothing to keep me from falling to the floor. They raised the foot of the bed and gave me oxygen. They rubbed me all over to get my circulation back. They did this it seemed like forever. I just wanted them to leave me alone and let me go to sleep. My veins had collapsed and they had trouble getting a vein to start an IV, as I was in shock from blood loss. I heard them say they would have to put it in my toe. I came alert enough to say "no, I have a good vein in my arm." They found a site and then gave me two units of blood that night and two more the next day.

Dr. Kearse told me if I had went to sleep that I might not have woke up. He said "those girls saved your life". I guess you would say I had a close call. It was the most relaxed and comfortable feeling and if that is how it is when you die I don't mind dying.

# Silver Dollars

When John was born an aunt of Bill's came to see him. She brought him a silver dollar with the year of his birth. When Jim was born she did the same thing. I have the coins in a safety deposit box for safe keeping. She must have lost interest, because Cindy and David didn't get one.

# Pony-tail

Imagine me with a pony tail! Well, I had one. My hair hung down my back. I spent a lot of time experimenting ways to wear it. It was not cut for over seven years. Mostly because I didn't have time to get perms or haircuts. Too much to do! It really never entered my mind.

One day I was at the drug store getting a sick baby some medicine. I had to wait for it and I was looking around the store. The clerk told me that every time I turned my head my hair was getting in the baby's face. I was holding it in my arms, over my shoulder. I had no idea that was happening. My long hair was easier to take care of than short hair. I liked to put a bun on the top of my head at the back. It stayed well and stayed off of my neck. This was really nice in the hot summer months.

# Wall Figures

Wallace, my brother, used to come to see me sometimes on Sunday afternoon. He would eat supper with me and the kids. Bill was usually at work. Wallace would play with the children . He liked to make designs on the wall with his hands and fingers. They were called shadow animals. Only John and Jim remember him. He loved children.

# Tadpoles

Up the road from our barn, in the spring, there was an area where rain would puddle and not dry. David discovered it was full of tadpoles. I bet there were hundreds. He came to the house and insisted I go to see them. Everyday when he got up, the first thing he did was to check on them. They grew their little legs and the next thing you knew they were tiny baby frogs. The process was fast and when they got old enough they were gone. Where did the frogs go??

# Intestinal Flu

While John was still a baby in his crib, he took the intestinal flu. This kind of flu was more known in the 50's than now. He would take his bottle and in about 30 minutes here it would come out in the form of diarrhea. The whole bed would have to be changed as it ran out of his diaper onto the sheets, gown and his blankets. I washed baby clothes every day for over a week to 10 days. He finally got over it. I usually just washed about 3 times a week under normal conditions.

# Chin Injury

When Jim was just crawling and learning to walk, he used to like to climb the steps. We were on the front porch one afternoon and he was going up and down the three concrete steps off of the porch. He was doing all right until one time he looked off and as he was coming back up the steps his hand missed the step and down went his head and his chin landed on the edge of the step. It made a gash about three inches long.

To the doctor we go. Bill took us in the truck. When we got to the doctor's office, Bill took Jim in and I stayed with John in the truck. All kinds of things ran through my mind. I could just see the doctor sewing with a needle and thread and sewing up the cut area. "Poor little Jim".

I could just see Jim and how it must be hurting. It was hot in that truck too, as there wasn't any air conditioner. Just what little air came in the window and that wasn't much as it was in the hot part of the day in July or August.

After about one hour, here they come. Happy as a lark!! Smiling. I asked how many stitches were taken and the reply was "none". The doctor had put a butterfly bandage on it to hold it together until it healed. It had to stay on for several days before it was to be taken off. It left a small scar that is still there today.

# Security Blanket

I can still see Jim today with his thumb in his mouth and holding on for dear life to his baby blanket. He would suck his thumb and hold his blanket in his hand and drag it around the house with him. He outgrew it before he went to school. It was washed every time any clothes were washed. "You played the dickens" trying to take it from him if he didn't want you to have it. He would cry until you had to give it back. I wish I had taken a picture of it but sometimes things get overlooked when you are busy.

# Birthday Party

The one and only birthday party I attempted to have was for John. I had a cake made at the bakery and had gotten the ice cream. I invited a few close relatives that lived close by. Well, a little boy in the neighborhood decided to ask some other children without first checking with me to see if it was all right. The room was full of all the stray children in the community. They devoured the whole cake and all of the ice cream. That was fine. When it got to the part where he opened his gifts he only got one besides the one we gave him. That sort of weaned me from parties. The object of a birthday party is to give gifts to the birthday person, right??

# Boots

Every Christmas Bill's routine was to take the boys to Asheville to get each a pair of boots. He got the best and he always took them late on Christmas Eve. They worked outside a lot and needed them for protection. Axes, power saws, snakes, mud holes, creeks, snow and other reasons, I can't remember, really put wear and tear on them. They usually lasted the year. I thought that was sweet of him to think of it as he wasn't much to give gifts. Many a Christmas Eve I waited to see if they got to the store before it closed. They made it every time. I did have several anxious moments sometimes.

# Cindy's Doll

Christmas time, Cindy always got a doll. However, she never really played with them. She just played outside swinging and riding a tricycle. One summer her doll disappeared. It was forgotten. After it turned cold and the leaves came off of the trees and bushes, I spied it one day in the very center of a big rose bush. No one knew how it got there. She did have a tough time growing up with three brothers. But she had never mentioned to me about it being gone. She did like Barbie dolls when she got older.

# Ducks

One Easter, the Easter Bunny brought two fluffy yellow ducks for the children. We kept them for several years. They made a nest on the creek bank in the Spring every year. They would lay their eggs there. The eggs were twice as big as a chicken egg. Those eggs made the lightest cake. The children enjoyed gathering them. They wouldn't leave them alone long enough to hatch.

One Spring the ducks disappeared. Bill said that they follow the water to find other ducks. So they probably just followed our creek and found a new home. We never saw them again.

# Slinging Statue

A neighbor boy was playing in our front yard with my three boys one afternoon. They were playing "slinging statue." This is where one person slings another person around and then turns him loose. You are to stand the way you are when you are turned loose. I heard Jim yell "Oh, you've broke my arm." Someone had slung him around and he fell on the edge of the walk, hitting his arm. Sure enough—to the doctor we go to get a cast applied. Jim said he felt the bone break when he fell.

# Head Injury

The children were playing at the creek one summer day. They were swimming and splashing each other. Cindy told David to stop splashing her, but he wouldn't quit. He was only about two years old. She picked up a tin can laying on the ground and threw it at him. She was only about five herself. Well, the can hit David above the eye and cut it. It started bleeding pretty bad.

One of the older boys decided that they had better bring him to the house for me to take care of him. Their Dad was in the bed sleeping as he was working the night shift. Here one of the boys come, I forgot which one, leading David by the hand. The other hand was over his eye with blood running between his fingers and still dripping to the floor. Of course, some of it was water mixed with the blood, and it was a pale pink. I looked at his eye and there was a gash about three inches long. To the doctor we go to get stitches in it. Children will be children.

By the way, I had to pay for doctor visits, no insurance paid for them in the 1950's. We had Champion insurance but it didn't cover office visits or medicine.

# Turtles

David, my youngest, loved the outdoors. He stayed at the creek every chance he got. He would lift up the rocks and grab whatever was under it. He caught red lizards, water snakes, and anything that moved. He arranged an aquarium that he put them in order to keep them. He put greenery, water, and rocks for the wiggley things to crawl on so they would not die. He would sell the lizards when people wanted them for fishing. I about fainted when one day I discovered a snake crawling around in it . As you can guess I had him remove the snake.

He also kept every turtle he could find. He had at least a dozen at one time. He made a little fenced in area so they could not get away but could crawl around in. He fed them nightcrawlers that he would pick up at night. He would hold the worm over their head and they would stand on their hind legs and stand up to get the worm. He taught me a lot about crawly things. He would put the nightcrawlers in a big 5-gallon can and cover them with straw. He would get my oatmeal and cornmeal and feed them. In the fall he would let the turtles go. He marked one to see if it came back the next year. Believe it or not he did find the turtle again.

In the fall I noticed the 5-gallon can still sitting in the yard. I tried to pick it up to move it and put it away. It was so heavy I could not budge it. I took the lid off and was I in for a surprise. It was crawling alive with the biggest fattest nightcrawlers you ever saw. Talk about getting the "willies"!! He had continued to feed them and they had multiplied and how. I believe he accidentally found a way to raise nightcrawlers.

# Mud Turtle

Bill took the boys on a walk in the adjoining pasture across from where we lived. He took them to a pond out of sight of the house and let them play and throw rocks in it for a while. Well— you know how kids get to putting sticks in the water to see what they can find. They found something all right. They found a huge mud turtle. It had to be an old one as it was really huge. It was still alive. Here they come with this giant turtle. It took two of them to carry it with a stick. Can you believe they wanted me to cook the thing. You guessed right. Again I said no thanks.

# Wild Strawberries

There was a large patch of wild strawberries down the road from our house in the pasture. One morning, I got up and cooked breakfast, then went to get the children up. David wasn't in his bed. He was only about three or four year old. I looked all over the house, in the barn and the yard, but no David. I called but no answer. I couldn't imagine where he was. We started eating and I kept going to the door to look for him.

Finally, I saw him coming up the road carrying a bowl very carefully. It would hold about a quart. When he got close enough to hear me, I asked him where he was. His reply was "I wanted some "prawberries" for my breakfast. He couldn't talk plain and he pronounced an "s" like a "p".

He had no idea the danger of this trip. He could have gotten snake bitten as the ground was covered with grass just high enough to hide a snake. And they do like strawberries. The wild strawberries are smaller than other strawberries and they have a taste all their own. His bowl was over ½ full. He was so proud of them. It had to have taken him over an hour to pick them. He had strawberries for his breakfast, with cream and sugar.

# Goats

Bill was forever surprising us when he came home. He never mentioned his plans. Here he would come with whatever it was. He drove a truck so there was no problem with hauling anything. He bought home a horse one day—that we named Fred. We kept him until he went blind about ten years later. He was hard to catch as he would run about the time they tried to put the halter on him. I had never been on a horse so one day when they had him out in the road riding him, I decided I wanted to try. Bill helped me up on the horse but I promptly got back down. I didn't like being at the mercy of that big animal. I felt like I was sitting on top of the barn, it was so high. That was the end of my horse back riding.

One day he bought home a kitten. That was the meanest cat. It wouldn't let you touch it. You could get your hand about to touch it and it would turn and scratch the heck out of you. It didn't stay with us long. He moved on.

One day he bought home some goats. I think there were two. He wanted them to eat what the horse or cows wouldn't. Goats eat almost anything but a horse and cow are picky what they eat. After about two weeks Jim's hands became cracked and sore. We took him to the doctor and he said he was allergic to the goats. So we gave them away. Bill had planned to make a little buggy for the goats to pull the children around in. We were disappointed but we soon got over it. Jim had to soak his hands in a purple medicine for them to get well.

# Cindy - Full Moon

When my daughter was born, it was Christmas and there was also a full moon. I couldn't sleep at night, so I would get up and look out the window at the moon to pass the night. I could see the old out-house by a tree, as it was as light as day.

It reminded me of a tale that Bill had told me about shooting a gun at the top of the building one day when he knew a boy was in there. He had seen him coming up the road and go in the building. When he shot the gun out came that boy pulling up his pants and yelling to "stop that"! I would stand and look at the moon until I got tired and went back to bed. Bill would be in the mill working.

The day before she was born I must have gotten what is referred to as the "nesting" instinct. I mopped all five floors in the house and then after they dried, I would wax them. I sat in a kitchen chair to mop and to wax the floors. I slid or scooted it around as I worked and still be sitting in it. I did this because I couldn't bend over very long as I had a lot of pressure because the baby was already overdue by over a week and I was very uncomfortable. It took about half a day

*Cindy with Bill, her Dad.*
*She is in her dance costume.*

to do it all. My daughter was born the next morning after only four hours of labor. They say you get a burst of energy before a baby is born, so I guess that is true.

# Cindy's Birth

Cindy was born on Christmas morning at 4:20. We went to the hospital in our Ford truck. We had to stop at Bill's mother to leave the two older boys. They did get to see that Santa Claus had come but that was all. On the way to town someone had left the lights on that were shining on a Santa Claus decoration on the lawn. He was pulling the sleigh and all. Bill said "look, boys, there is Santa Claus. He's on his way to someone else's house." Those little boys were really excited and to them that was really Santa Claus. They just kept looking at it until we were out of sight of it. This was about 1:30 a.m. after midnight.

When Cindy was born the doctor said "Oh Boy, I am going to get home in time to see my children get up to get their Santa gifts." When Cindy was born a nurse said to the doctor, "This is the 3rd red-headed baby this week, I'm beginning to get suspicious." She was kidding him! Cindy got her red hair from her Grandmother.

In the morning Bill took the boys back home to play with their toys. They had each gotten a tricycle and they rode them in the house. Jim said that they had a wreck by running into each other and cut Jim's leg with the fender. Bill promptly removed the fenders.

Bill's aunt that lived above us said she looked out and here came Bill and he looked liked he was floating on air, he was so proud. He was on "cloud nine". He came in and said "well, we got a little old girl." She said the smile on his face told a thousand words. He was proud as could be of that little girl. Red hair and all!

# Cindy

I heard Cindy crying one day. She had just learned to talk. My children always played outside unless it was too cold or was raining. I looked out to see what was wrong. She had wandered off across the road and down near a long row of grape vines. I called to her and asked her what was wrong. She was crying and pointing and saying "Gobble – Gobble." There stood the biggest turkey and it was coming straight toward her. She was frozen to the spot. Her brothers ran up and shooed it away. I don't know who it belonged to or where it came from. I know it wasn't ours. My children played outside as soon as they could walk.

# Oxygen Tent

When David, my youngest son, was about eighteen months old he got the croup or what we call today bronchitis. It developed quick. He woke me up one night crying and was choked up a little. I got him back to sleep. The next day he slept a lot and didn't eat much. The second night he kept me up all night crying and was "choked up" again like he couldn't breathe well. My husband was at the mill working the night shift. He was off the next day.

Well, that day by ten o'clock he couldn't take a bottle as he would lose his breath and have to quit and he would cry. I told my husband that he needed to go to the doctor. It was a Sunday. We called Dr. Moore as he was the only doctor we could find to see him. He checked him and got concerned that he might have diphtheria as he had a sister who had died from it. He immediately sent us to the hospital with him and had him put under a Oxygen tent. I stayed with him and my husband went home to stay with the other children and to do the outside work and feeding of the cows, dogs and pigs.

We had left the children with a friend of Bill's that was there when I told him the baby was sick. I sat by the Oxygen tent and bed all afternoon until Dr. Moore came up to check on him. He asked how he was. I told him that I had noticed every now and then David would look dark or cyanotic and his lips would turn purple. His fingernails also turned dark. I thought this was unusual with him under the tent getting oxygen. He shouldn't be doing that.

The doctor left the room and about ten minutes later I heard fast walking footsteps coming down the hall to our room. In came Dr. Moore with Dr. Doris Hammett, a pediatrician. She looked at David and turned to me and said "where is your husband?" I didn't know why she was asking me that. I said, "At home." She said "well, call him and get him up here." She looked at Dr. Moore and said "I'm taking this baby now to put in a trache without a permit. They can sign it when her husband gets here, this can't wait."

With that she picked up the baby and down the hall she went carrying David in her arms. When he came back to the room she had performed a tracheotomy (a tube placed in the throat to allow air to pass to the lungs.). We had to have private nurses with him for ten days of the two weeks he stayed in the hospital.

Bill stayed in the day time and I went at night. Someone had to stay at home with the other three children. Bill took a two week vacation to be available. I stayed at night even though there was a nurse with him.

We had to be at his side all the time because we never knew when the trachea would block off with thick secretions. They had to be suctioned out and the trachea cleaned. If we didn't he couldn't breathe.

All this happened before I.V.'s were put in the vein. The medicine was injected slowly directly into the flesh. It was given in his thigh. It would make his leg so heavy you could hardly lift it. It would just get absorbed and here they came with another one. He also had penicillin shots in the buttocks. I counted over fifty marks where he had had injections that were still visible. I don't know how many had already disappeared.

He was a scared little boy. He looked frightened when I came in the room. There was a picture of a horse in a field that hung at the head of the bed and when he got to feeling better he would point to it when I came in the room and say "Horsey, Horsey." It really got to his dad. He would help by bathing him and sitting with him all day.

David still has the small scar at his throat to show of his ordeal. I found out later that another baby from our area was also admitted for the same thing but only had to stay a couple of days. It wasn't as sick as David was — croup develops fast. David was never made to work on the farm as much as the other boys. His dad just felt so sorry for him when he was sick he didn't have the heart to be hard on him. We nearly lost him.

# Best Citizen

When Jim was still in grammar school at Beaverdam, he insisted that I come to a program they were having one morning. I asked him why it was so important and he told me that he thought his best friend, Bob, was going to be honored at the meeting. He seemed to think that Bob had been selected as the Best Citizen.

Well, I went and all through the program I kept thinking that Bob was going to get the honor. They called the winners out for the rooms and it was Jim from his room. I thought well, he won for the room and Bob won for the school. Was I ever surprised when they called out Jim's name for the school! He had won for both the room and the school. He was really surprised and so was I. I wonder if he knew he had won as they had kept it a secret from him. I was so proud of him.

# Little Drummer Boy

One Christmas Jim asked me to come to a play that his class was putting on for the Christmas holidays. When I got there and it started, who was the Little Drummer Boy?? You guessed it. It was Jim. He had the lead part!

# Family

I keep referring to my older brother. Well, I really had four brothers. William the oldest died in the fall before he would have graduated from high school in the following spring. He had an inner ear infection that was referred to back then as a rising in the ear. Antibiotics weren't available then. They say our house was "run over" with neighbors and friends as he was so well liked.

The next year my oldest sister, Louise, died from a ruptured appendix and peritonitis. They were the two oldest children in the family. Imagine having a set of twins in January and in the fall loosing your oldest son and then the following year to loose your oldest daughter. Talk about misfortunes!!

This made Wallace my next brother in line to become the oldest living child in the family. I was just a baby when both William and Louise died, so I don't remember either of them. I understand that William played with us when he came home from school. We were about nine months old when he died.

During World War II all of my brothers served in the military. My then older brother, Wallace, joined the Navy the Monday after Japan attached Pearl Harbor. He had only been married about a week. He was gone from home for over two years and only coming into New York harbor long enough to re-load the ship and then back to sea.

When he came home after the war, we were all excited. The day he was due home we watched the road to see if he was coming yet. If it wasn't our mom it was us looking. We finally decided they had made a mistake and he wasn't coming after all. So Tommie and I went out to play.

We were in the back yard playing when we heard the most awful sound from the house—screaming, crying and just a racket in general. Talk about scaring two little girls. Well, it was my mom welcoming home Wallace from the Navy. My mom loved him and we all knew that he was her favorite. We were disappointed that we missed seeing him come out the road home.

Roy was my next oldest brother and he served in the Marines but he didn't see active duty. Buzz, my third brother was in the Army, and he didn't see combat either.

Top: William Paxton (oldest child)—Died in 1929.

Left: Louise Paxton (second child)—Died in 1930.

When Wallace, the brother in the Navy came home on leave he would get us to wash his white uniform. He would give us 50 cents, to wash it and he would show us how. We had to wash it in the bathtub very carefully. That was his way of giving us money to spend. He made us earn it. After he wore it he would then let my twin sister wash it too. Everyone tried to treat us alike.

Now—Roy my next oldest brother would give us an allowance every payday after he got a job in the mill. He was very proud of the twins. He would give us each 50 cents a piece—just for ourselves. He always carried a picture in his billfold all the time of us.

We used to take him milk to the apartment where he lived with his first wife. Our mom milked a cow and she let him have milk. One day he took our picture in the parking lot there. It was an awful picture but he carried it faithfully in his billfold and never hesitated to take it out and show it off.

After he bought a car he would let us play in it and pretend to drive. I guess that helped us later when we did drive. He walked to work because we lived so close to the mill. Wallace had a car also. His had a "rumble seat" in it. He used to take us for a ride in it. My twin, Tommie, my sister Winnie and myself sat in the rumble seat with the wind blowing our hair. Winnie's job was to keep us from falling out. Those were the days!!

I can't leave out my last brother. He bought us our first pair of skates. We also learned to ride a bike by sneaking out his while he was at work. He usually kept a chain and lock on it but we would check it everyday and if he had forgotten to put the lock on it we got that sucker out and rode it. Children will be children.

# Remembering Wallace, Roy, And Buzz (Burlin) My Brothers

Wallace was our Mom's favorite child. We think it was mostly because Mom favored him and Daddy was jealous of him. He was the oldest child after the other older brother and sister died. He liked to fish. He was a handsome boy with dark hair and was about six feet tall. He had lots of girl friends in school. He went to the Navy after Pearl Harbor was attacked. He had just gotten married the week before. I remember him and my parents listening to the radio and hearing about the attack. He played football in high school and I believe it was the first football team for Canton High School. It was just getting started.

He used to visit me in the country after I married. He would eat supper with me and play with my children. Only John and Jim, my oldest remember him. He lived down the road from us for a while. He bought sweet milk from me. He had a bad stomach brought on from stress from his "stint" in the service. Two different ships he was on were attacked and one was sunk out from under him. He saw buddies of his killed and drowned. He died at age 42 from a heart attack.

I remember when he was a boy he would bring friends home and they would eat supper with us. One time one of them asked for a biscuit and he just threw it across the table to him. So "throwed rolls" concept isn't new!! Dad wasn't there or he probably would have corrected them. Our house was always open to friends of the children.

# Roy

Roy was next in line to Wallace. Roy was always proud of his little twin sisters. He carried our pictures in his billfold for years. He would let us play in his car while he was at work and we would pretend to drive. We didn't hurt the car as we were careful.

One day he told Tommie and me that he was going to take us to see our Grandma and Grandpa Jones at Balsam the next day. He wanted us to dress up nice and wash our hair. We left early in the morning. We drove down the road and he said he needed to go somewhere else first. So he goes to the Thickety community. It was on the other side of the mill. Tommie and I sat in the car while he went in.

After a bit he came out and told us to get out and come into the house. There was someone he wanted us to meet. It was a girl and her parents. We got in the car and started to Grandmas when "Dude" announced that we couldn't go to Grandmas today as he had to go somewhere else first. He promised to take us another time. So he took us home. We were disappointed but we soon got over it.

We learned later that he had gone to South Carolina that day and had gotten married. He just had his future bride and her family to see us. As I say he was proud of his twin sisters. He never did take us to Grandmas to make up for it. I guess he forgot. He worked at Champion.

# Buzz-Burlin-Joe

There were two girls born and then Buzz came along. As children we used to sit on the ground and play mumbly peg with Winnie and Buzz. They played with us a lot.

Buzz was a worker. He mowed yards at an early age. When he got older he got a job with the post office to carry the mail during the summer vacation. People along the way would give him cold lemonade on hot days. He had to walk all over town carrying the mail in a mail sack on his back. He had a short leg as the result of falling

*Wallace, Burlin-"Buzz" in the middle Roy "Dude" on right near the window, Daddy in the chair in front.*

*Opposing page: My sisters and I—Dee, Tommie, Jo, and Winnie.*

down the front concrete steps as a child and breaking his leg. It didn't heal properly.

He courted the girls and brought home jewelry they would give him. He kept them in a cigar box. As a boy he collected butterflies to dry and then pin them to paper. It was a scout project. He also made model airplanes and cars from kits and played with an erector set. He made a running ferris wheel one time from it. It ran with an electric motor. He was always busy.

He went to college and made an engineer. The bicycle I learned to ride on was his. He was never mean to the girls in the family as were neither of the other two boys. We got along pretty good as families go.

# Remembering My Sisters

First, my oldest sister, Louise, died young before she finished school from complications from appendicitis. Another sister died at nine months old. That left me with two other sisters and my twin, Tommie.

Annie Dee was the oldest left living sister. She helped my mom to keep the house clean. She dusted the furniture and swept and mopped the floors every morning. We didn't get in the house when this was going on. She'd mop the floors and she would not let us walk

on them until they dried. The house stayed spotless with her care. She would lock the screen door and we knew to stay away.

Winnie, I am told was Daddy's pet. She was a petite dark eyed girl with dark hair. I remember she wouldn't let us twins around when her friends came to visit. We were too young. Dee and Winnie were very smart in school and went on to college and made four year RNs.

My twin Tommie, went to college and then worked for Champion for a short period of time until she got married. I just kept on working as I had since I was 15. I knew it would be hard for my dad to send us both to college at the same time. I really didn't want to go anyway. He offered to send me to Asheville to a small business school but I didn't care about it. I ended up getting married before Tommie finished college.

These sisters with myself are all that's still living out of a family of ten. Katrina was the sister who died as an infant.

# My Parents

My father, born in 1886, remembered as a boy of nine traveling by covered wagon with his parents from Transylvania County

*My Parents*

through Wagon Road Gap to Waynesville, his new home. He married Annie Jones in 1909 and moved to Canton to work for the Champion Paper plant for the next 42 years.

In his early twenties his leg was severely injured in a plant accident and resulted in one leg being shorter than the other one. This caused him to limp slightly and earned him the nickname of "Shorty". Their family of ten were all born at home. The last born was a set of twin girls.

# My Mom

She was noted for her quick smile and her willingness to help others, color was no barrier. She loved to trade flowers and plants with her friends. She sold Christmas cards door to door for several years. I think it was more to be with friends than the money. She was very devoted to her church.

She loved to quilt in her spare time. She left over 50 quilts that were completely quilted when she died, plus at least 20 quilt tops she had put together. Her friends gave her scraps of cloth and she had bags of them. Among some of the quilts were the Dutch Boy and the Wedding Ring design. One quilt was made from old wool material and was it heavy and warm.

# My Dad

He is remembered mostly, I guess, for his short leg that caused him to limp slightly. As I mentioned earlier that he was hurt in the mill and was out of work for about a year for the leg to heal. This happened during the depression, I was told when I was still a baby. I am sure it was very hard on the family with ten children and twin babies at that.

He liked his pipe and it wasn't far from him very often. He kept it and a tobacco pouch in his pocket. To my knowledge he was never burned from it. He worked until he was 68 years old, when Social Security came along and more or less made him retire. He lived 20 years after that.

# Grandma and Grandpa Jones

My Grandma Jones, my mother's mother was sick for a long time before she died. She was sick and in bed the whole summer before she died. My mom stayed with her and she kept us with her (my twin and I). She lived at Balsam, a community above Waynesville, N. C.

We played in the woods, climbing trees and playing with a cousin named Betty. She lived with her mother in a house close to our grandparents.

We went to church with Granddaddy Jones. We went to church on Sunday and then again on Wednesday for prayer meeting. He

*William Henderson Jones and his wife, Cenie Bailes Jones.*

preached sometimes when the regular preacher couldn't be there. He was also the Sunday School Superintendent at the little white country church. He made us mind and pay attention in church.

When Grandma Jones died my mom couldn't decide whether to let us see her in her coffin or not. Finally, she decided she would do it because we needed to see a dead person sometime and it might as well be now. She got us by the hand and told us to just look quick and look away and not to panic. Being told this made my legs weak and my heart beat faster. I couldn't feel my legs as they moved. My Grandma didn't look like herself and she looked white and pastey pale. I dreamed about it several times after it happened.

A week after she was buried, my mom's brother died suddenly from a heart attack. She screamed and screamed when they called and told her. He was her favorite brother.

Every spring my mom would give us a run of worm medicine. We called it "wormy fudge". It was made from Jerusalem Oak and mixed with molasses. I hated that stuff. She'd make us sit down in a chair in front of her and stay there until we had swallowed it.

One time we went outside and spit it out and a tattle tale told on us so from then on we had to be monitored when we took it. We were the only ones to take it because "they were too old". It was thick and gooey and it made you gag. She also used to make us take cod liver oil for our health, also. I remember taking the worm medicine at Balsam one time.

Grandpa Jones was a barber. He cut soldiers hair during World War I. He went with his boys to war and stayed in camp with them.

# Paxton Grandparents

I don't remember my Dad's parents (Grandpa and Grandma Paxton). They died before I could remember them. I was told that she died first. She was 67 years old and died in August 1919. He died later of congestive heart failure. He had to sleep sitting up in a chair because he couldn't breathe laying down. He was 79 years old when he died in 1931. I was only two at the time. Surviving family members put up their grave marker as he left no money for it. They are buried in Old Locust Field Cemetery at the end of the concrete walk across the road from where Pennsylvania Avenue School stood and now stands the Library.

*Above: Grandpa Paxton.*
*Right: My Dad with Grandma Paxton.*

# FAMILY TREE (WOOD - PAXTON)

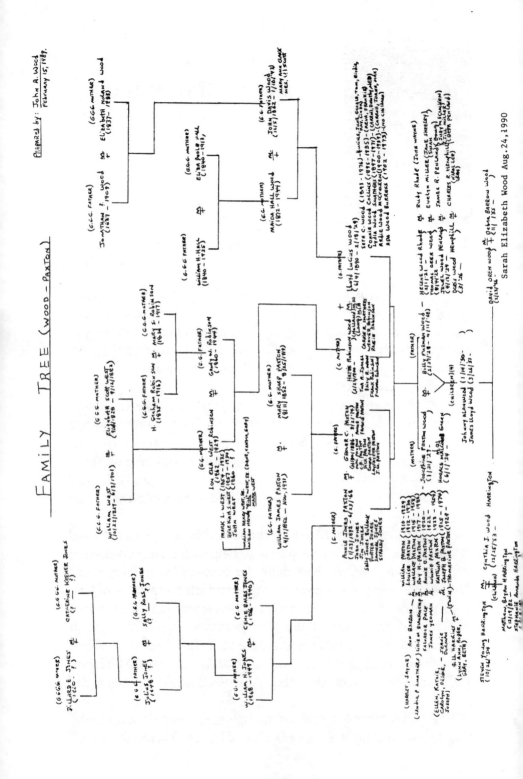

PREPARED BY: John A. Wood
FEBRUARY 15, 1989.

Sarah Elizabeth Wood Aug. 24, 1990

# About the Author

Josephine was one of twins born during the depression of 1929. They were raised in the town of Canton and went to school there. They had everything a town had to offer—such as paved streets, inside bathrooms, street lights and a big house with an upstairs. Her childhood was a good one but some heartaches also showed up now and then.

At 19 she married and moved to North Hominy to a small farm in the country. This farm was about 30 acres. The house was the one her husband was raised in. She didn't even know there was a place called Hominy until she was a senior in high school. She went out there with a friend one day. Her life was hard in Canton, N. C., and even harder in the country, but she enjoyed it and looked at it as an adventure.

Her husband's father had died when the child was just a baby and before Social Security was available to help with raising children of widows. His mother worked about the community on dairy farms that were thriving at the time. Her husband left her a piece of land and a total of $50 cash. She had a small two-room house built to live in. The neighbors would bring in potatoes, apples and sweet potatoes when they were gathered and if they had extra. They shared pork when pigs were slaughtered and apples would find their way to their front porch after dark. Also wood would show up in the yard.

When his mother got a job at Champion, she added rooms to the little house making it a three-bedroom house. This is the house where Josephine moved and raised her family until her own husband's death at age 40, leaving her a widow with four children at age 39. She then moved back to town. She stayed and raised the children until the last one was in his last year of college.

She chose to go back to school to learn a trade to support herself. She chose nursing because she had worked part-time as an aide in a local nursing home and liked the work. She also figured there would always be sick people and a job. She went to Haywood Technical College and it was a new adventure, as she had been out of school over 20 years.

After getting her Nurse's License she went to work at the local hospital in Haywood County. She worked long after retirement as hard work didn't slow her down. She still works as this book is being written.

She was always telling crazy stories about things that happened to her after she moved to the country. Her son Jim said that since he didn't know any of these stories, he would like her to write them down. When she couldn't sleep at night she would get up and write down a memory that would come to her. You can see that she didn't waste her time. This is how this book came about. Times of old need to be recorded for future generations. Some lessons can be learned from some of the adventures.